PRIMARY MATHEMATICS 1B

WORKBOOK

U.S. EDITION

Marshall Cavendish
Education

SM SingaporeMath.com Inc®

Original edition published under the titles
Primary Mathematics Workbook 1B (Part One) and 1B (Part Two)
© 1981 Curriculum Planning & Development Division
Ministry of Education, Singapore
Published by Times Media Private Limited
This American Edition
© 2003 Times Media Private Limited
© 2003 Marshall Cavendish International (Singapore) Private Limited

Published by Marshall Cavendish Education
An imprint of Marshall Cavendish International (Singapore) Private Limited
Times Centre, 1 New Industrial Road, Singapore 536196
Customer Service Hotline: (65) 6411 0820
E-mail: tmesales@sg.marshallcavendish.com
Website: www.marshallcavendish.com/education

SingaporeMath.com Inc®
Distributed by
SingaporeMath.com Inc
404 Beavercreek Road #225
Oregon City, OR 97045
U.S.A.
Website: www.singaporemath.com

First published 2003
Reprinted 2003, 2004 (twice)
Second impression 2005
Reprinted 2005 (twice), 2006 (thrice), 2007 (twice), 2008, 2009 (twice),
          2010 (twice), 2011 (twice)

ISBN 978-981-01-8497-1

Printed in Singapore by Times Printers, www.timesprinters.com

ACKNOWLEDGEMENTS

Our special thanks to Richard Askey, Professor of Mathematics (University of Wisconsin,
Madison), Yoram Sagher, Professor of Mathematics (University of Illinois, Chicago), and Madge
Goldman, President (Gabriella and Paul Rosenbaum Foundation), for their indispensable
advice and suggestions in the production of Primary Mathematics (U.S. Edition).

CONTENTS

4   Multiplication

9 Money

EXERCISE 1

1. Write Yes or No.

(a)

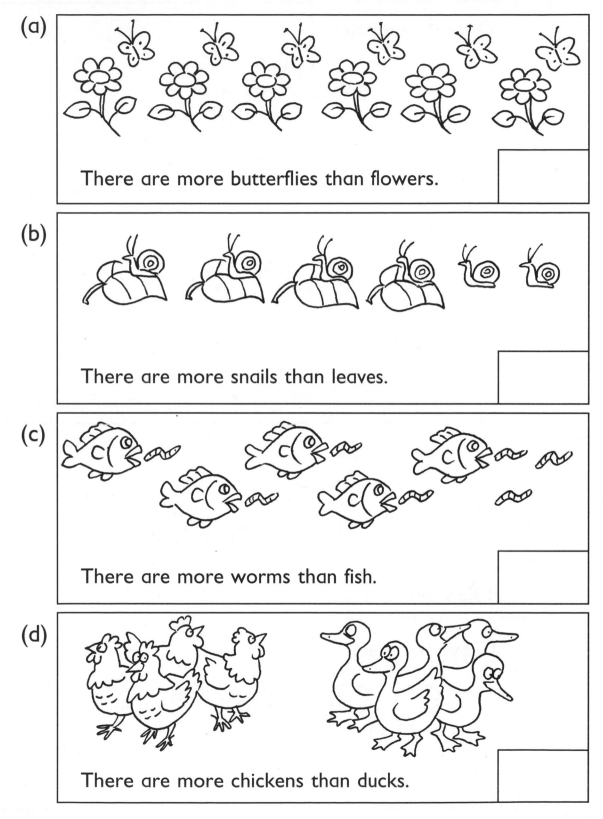

There are more butterflies than flowers.

(b)

There are more snails than leaves.

(c)

There are more worms than fish.

(d)

There are more chickens than ducks.

EXERCISE 2

1. (a)

Draw 1 more star.

1 more than 7 is _____.

(b)

Draw 1 more flower.

1 more than 5 is _____.

2. (a)

Cross out 1 bottle.

1 less than 8 is _____.

(b)

Cross out 1 leaf.

1 less than 9 is _____.

3. Join each balloon to the correct answer.

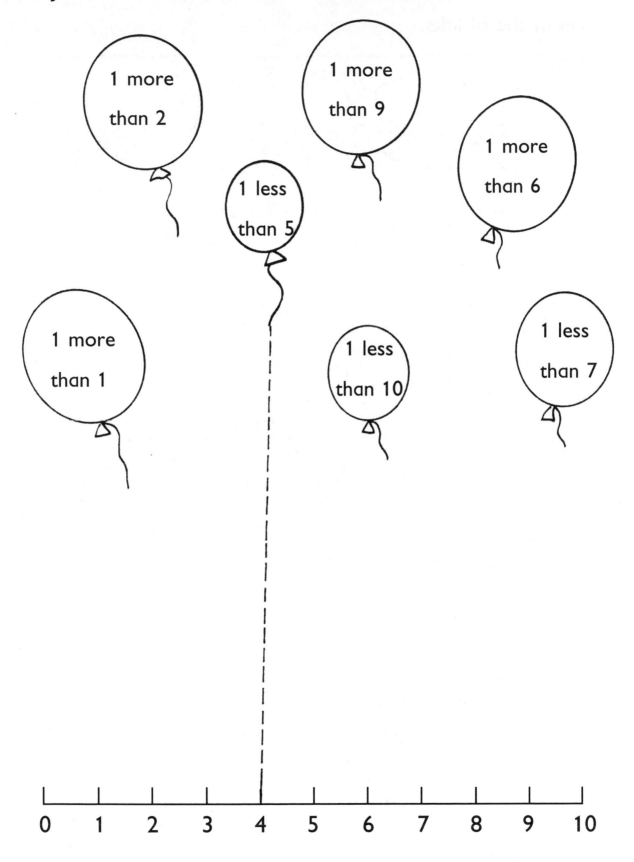

EXERCISE 3

1. Fill in the blanks.

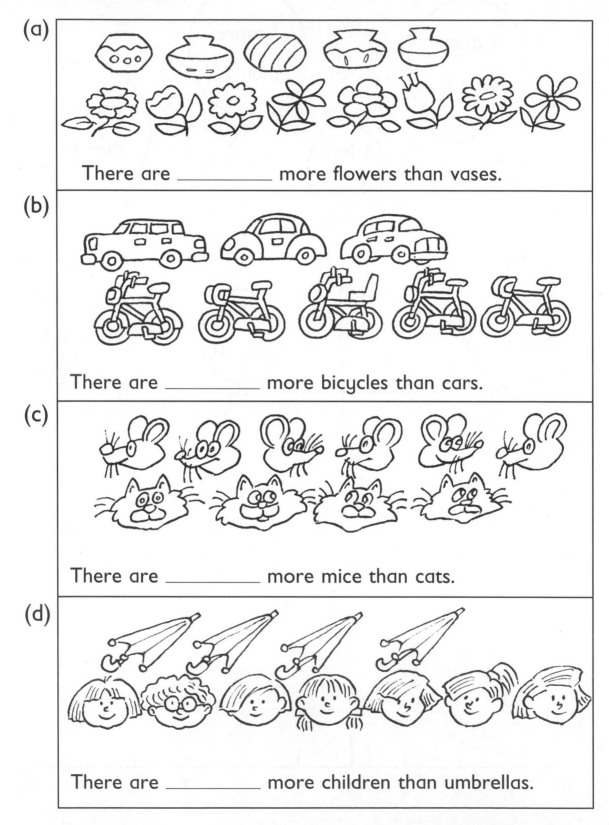

(a) There are _____ more flowers than vases.

(b) There are _____ more bicycles than cars.

(c) There are _____ more mice than cats.

(d) There are _____ more children than umbrellas.

2. Fill in the blanks.

Matthew's balls   Peter's balls

_____ has more balls.

He has _____ more balls.

Lily's buttons   Dani's buttons

_____ has more buttons. She has _____ more buttons.

Ryan's toy boats   Ian's toy boats

Ryan has _____ more toy boats than Ian.

Sara's beads   Taylor's beads

Sara has _____ fewer beads than Taylor.

EXERCISE 4

1.

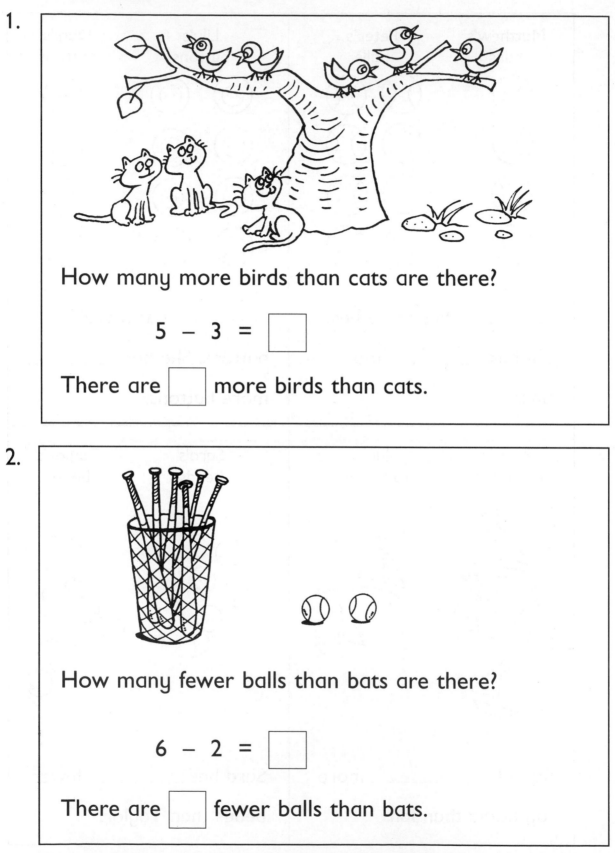

How many more birds than cats are there?

5 – 3 = ☐

There are ☐ more birds than cats.

2.

How many fewer balls than bats are there?

6 – 2 = ☐

There are ☐ fewer balls than bats.

3.

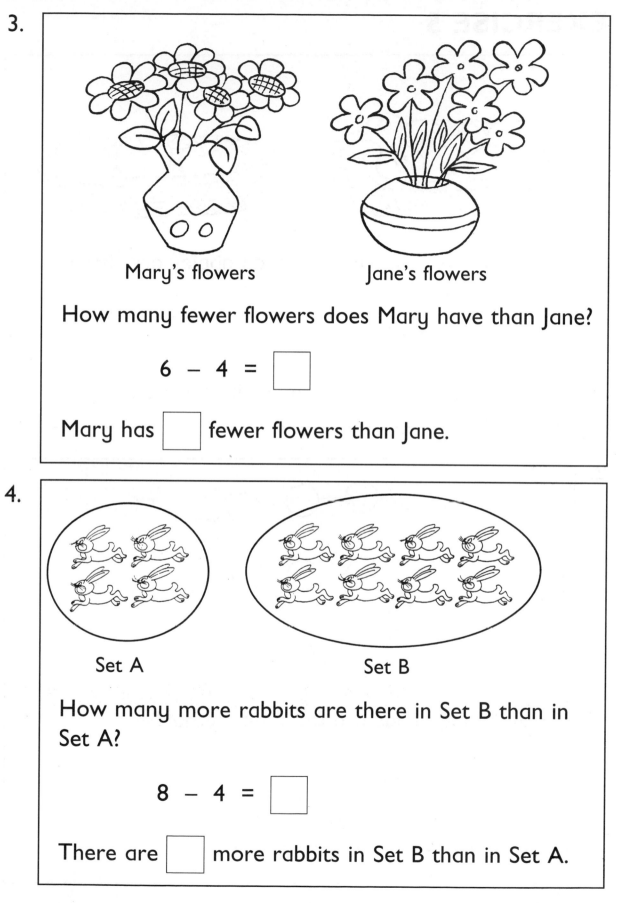

Mary's flowers   Jane's flowers

How many fewer flowers does Mary have than Jane?

6 − 4 = ☐

Mary has ☐ fewer flowers than Jane.

4.

Set A   Set B

How many more rabbits are there in Set B than in Set A?

8 − 4 = ☐

There are ☐ more rabbits in Set B than in Set A.

EXERCISE 5

1.

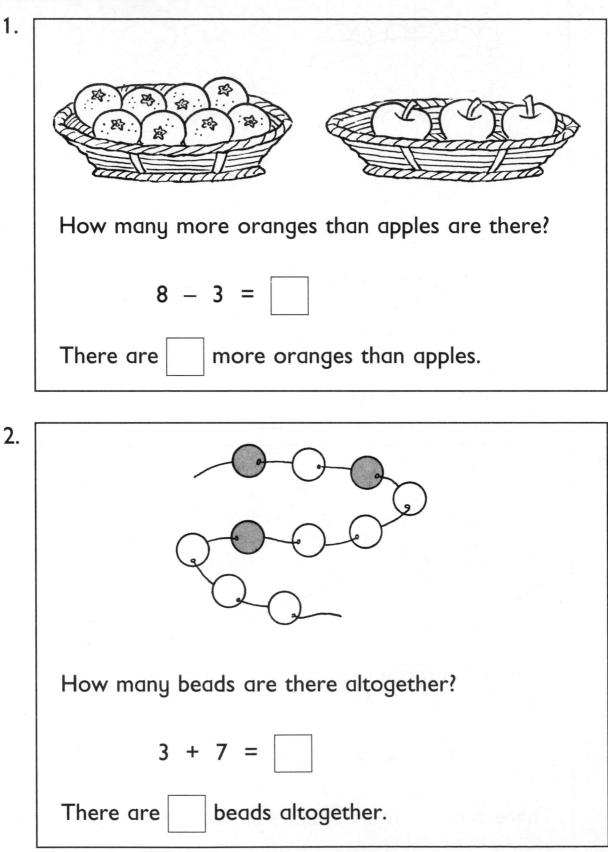

How many more oranges than apples are there?

8 − 3 = ☐

There are ☐ more oranges than apples.

2.

How many beads are there altogether?

3 + 7 = ☐

There are ☐ beads altogether.

3.

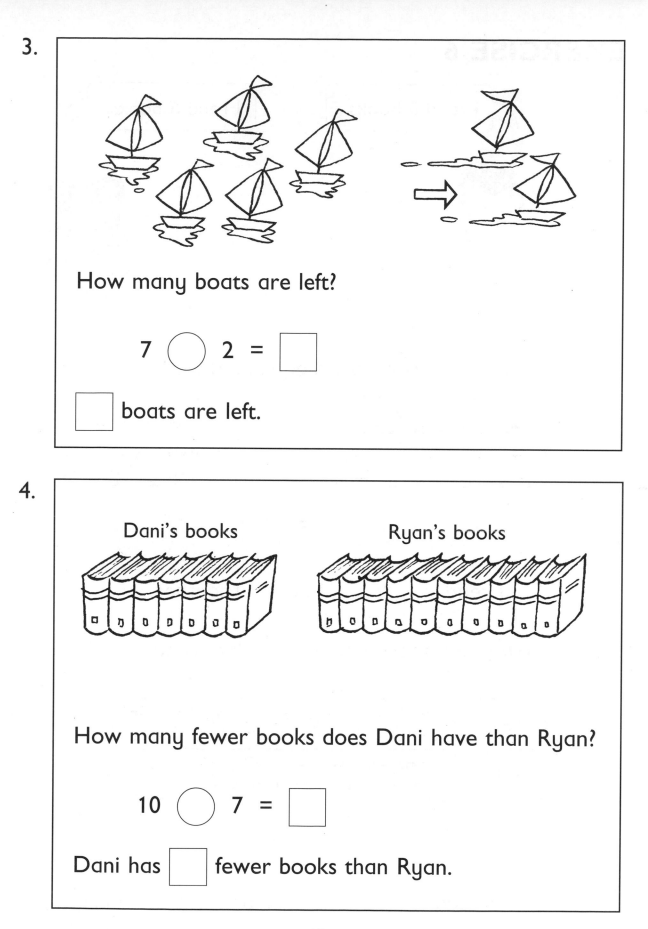

How many boats are left?

7 ◯ 2 = ☐

☐ boats are left.

4.

Dani's books　　　　Ryan's books

How many fewer books does Dani have than Ryan?

10 ◯ 7 = ☐

Dani has ☐ fewer books than Ryan.

EXERCISE 6

1.

(a) How many books did they read altogether?

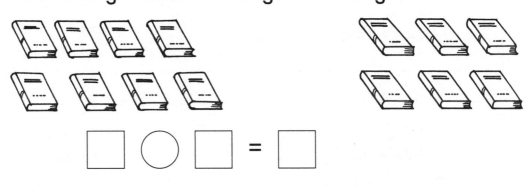

□ ◯ □ = □

They read _____ books altogether.

(b) How many more books did Adam read than Haley?

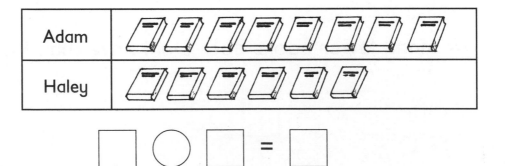

Adam	
Haley	

□ ◯ □ = □

Adam read _____ more books than Haley.

2.

I have 4 pencils. — Susan

I have 3 pencils. — Jamie

How many pencils do they have altogether?

☐ ◯ ☐ = ☐

They have ☐ pencils altogether.

3.

I have 8 marbles. — Joe

I have 2 marbles. — John

How many more marbles does Joe have than John?

☐ ◯ ☐ = ☐

Joe has ☐ more marbles than John.

EXERCISE 7

1.

At a Toy Shop

| Car | Drum | Boat |

Fill in the blanks.

(a) There are _____ cars.

(b) There are _____ drums.

(c) There are _____ boats.

(d) There are _____ toys altogether.

(e) There are _____ more boats than drums.

Raju's Pets

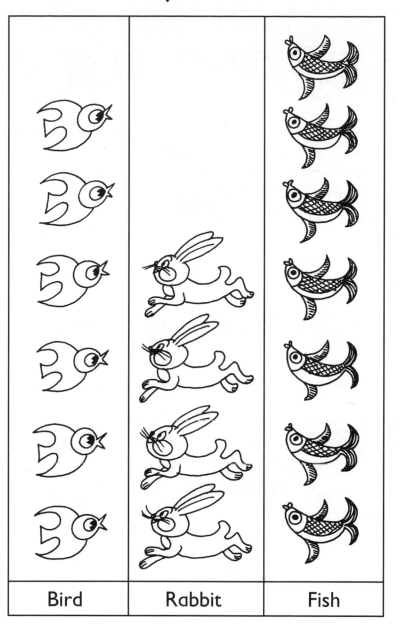

| Bird | Rabbit | Fish |

Fill in the blanks.

(a) Raju has _____ rabbits.

(b) He has _____ birds.

(c) He has _____ more fish than rabbits.

(d) He has _____ fewer rabbits than birds.

3. At the Zoo

Monkey	
Lion	
Bear	

Fill in the blanks.

(a) There are _____ monkeys.

(b) There are _____ bears.

(c) There are _____ more monkeys than bears.

(d) There are _____ fewer lions than bears.

(e) There are _____ animals altogether.

EXERCISE 8

1.

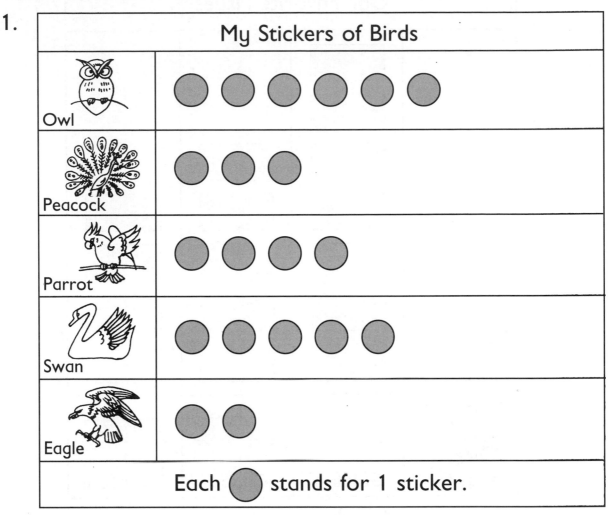

My Stickers of Birds

Each ◯ stands for 1 sticker.

Fill in the blanks.

(a) There are _____ stickers altogether.

(b) There are _____ stickers of swans.

(c) There are _____ more stickers of owls than of parrots.

(d) There are _____ fewer stickers of eagles than of swans.

(e) The number of stickers of _____ is the greatest.

(f) The number of stickers of _____ is the smallest.

2.

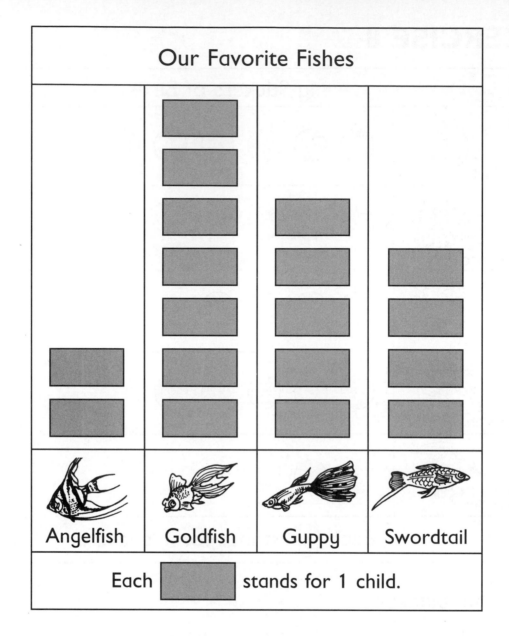

Fill in the blanks.

(a) _____ children like goldfish best.

(b) _____ children like swordtails best.

(c) _____ more children like guppies than angelfish.

(d) _____ fewer children like swordtails than goldfish.

(e) The least popular fish is _____.

(f) The most popular fish is _____.

EXERCISE 9

1.

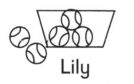
Lily

Ali

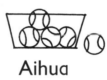
Aihua

Peter

Count the balls in each basket.

Then complete this graph.

Lily	⚾	⚾	⚾				
Ali							
Aihua							
Peter							

2. The picture shows the toys in a shop.

   Count each type of toy and complete the graph below.

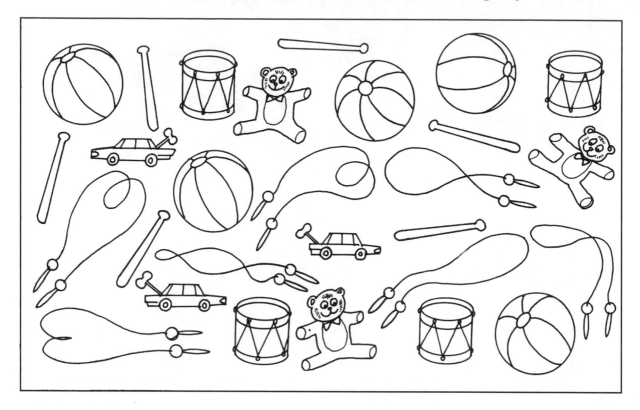

Toys at a Shop

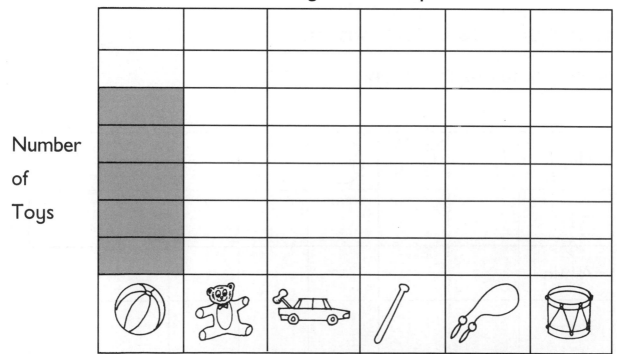

Number of Toys

EXERCISE 10

1. Circle groups of 10. Then count and write the number.

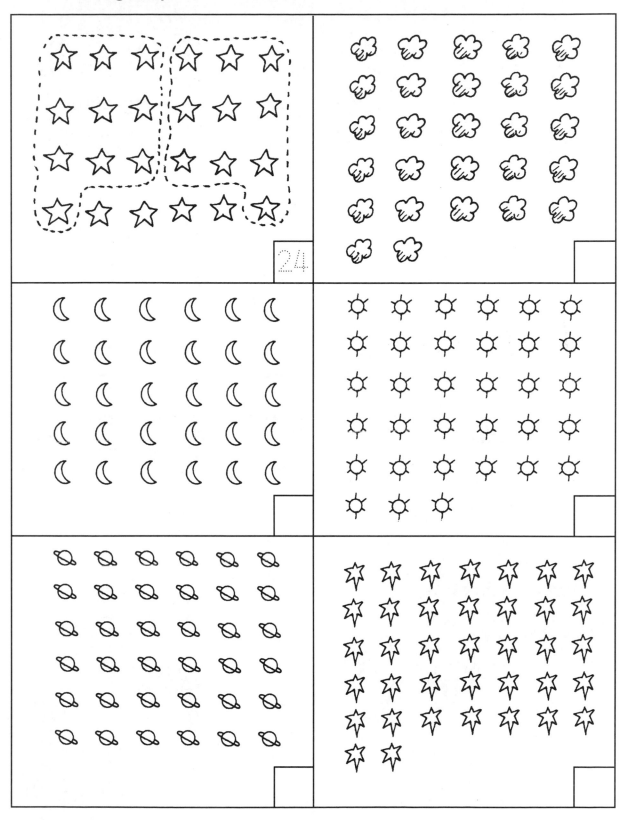

EXERCISE 11

1. Match.

2. Write the numbers.

thirty-six

twenty-five

thirty-nine

thirty-two

thirty

thirty-four

twenty-eight

twenty-seven

twenty-four

thirty-three

EXERCISE 12

1. Fill in the missing numbers.

   (a)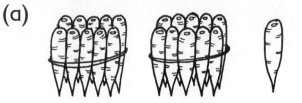

   1 more than 20 is _____.

   (b)

   3 more than 30 is _____.

   (c)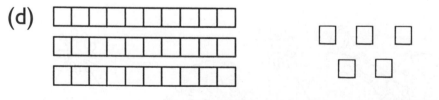

   6 more than 20 is _____.

   (d)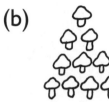

   5 more than 30 is _____.

EXERCISE 13

1. Fill in the missing numbers.

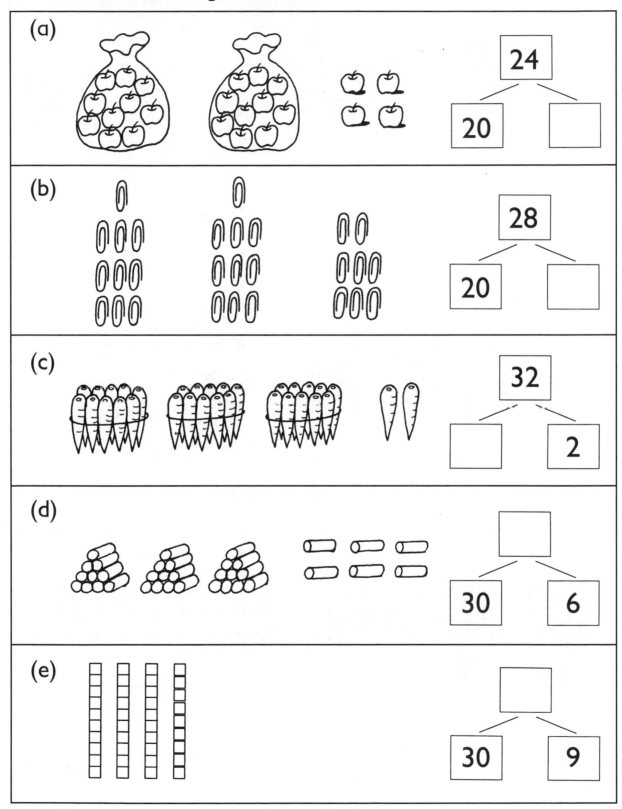

(a)

24

20 ☐

(b)

28

20 ☐

(c)

32

☐ 2

(d)

☐

30 6

(e)

☐

30 9

2. Fill in the missing numbers.

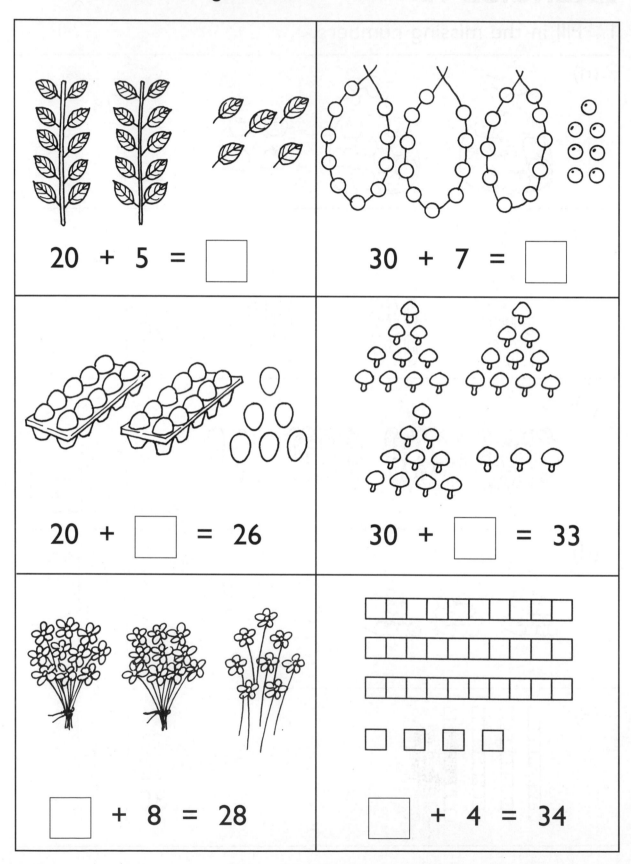

20 + 5 = [ ]

30 + 7 = [ ]

20 + [ ] = 26

30 + [ ] = 33

[ ] + 8 = 28

[ ] + 4 = 34

EXERCISE 14

1. Fill in the missing numbers.

(a)

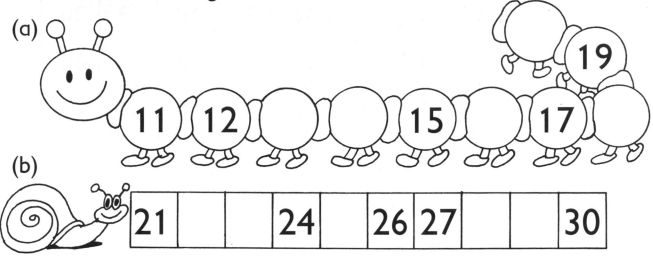

11 12 ☐ ☐ 15 ☐ 17 ☐ 19

(b)

21			24		26	27			30

(c)

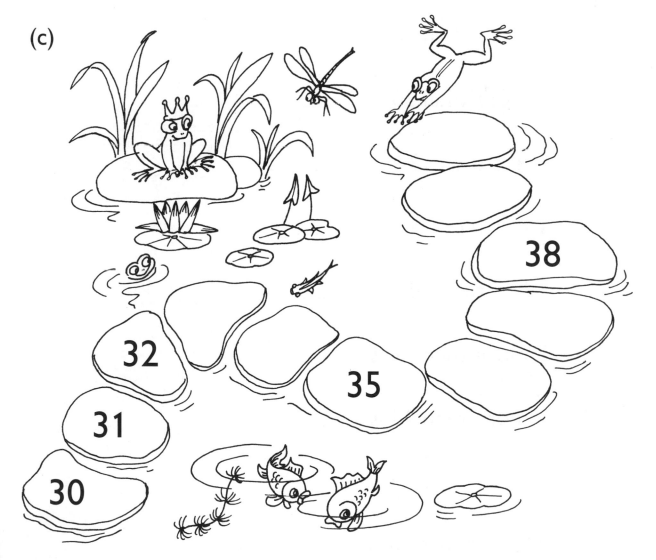

38

32

35

31

30

31

1	2	3	4	5	6	7	8	9	10
11	12	13	14	15	16	17	18	19	20
21	22	23	24	25	26	27	28	29	30
31	32	33	34	35	36	37	38	39	40

2. Fill in the blanks.

(a) 1 more than 15 is _____.

(b) 1 more than 26 is _____.

(c) 1 more than 30 is _____.

(d) 1 less than 18 is _____.

(e) 1 less than 33 is _____.

(f) 1 less than 40 is _____.

(g) 2 more than 17 is _____.

(h) 2 more than 29 is _____.

(i) 2 less than 28 is _____.

(j) 2 less than 37 is _____.

EXERCISE 15

1. Use the numbers in the bag to fill in the blanks.

(a)

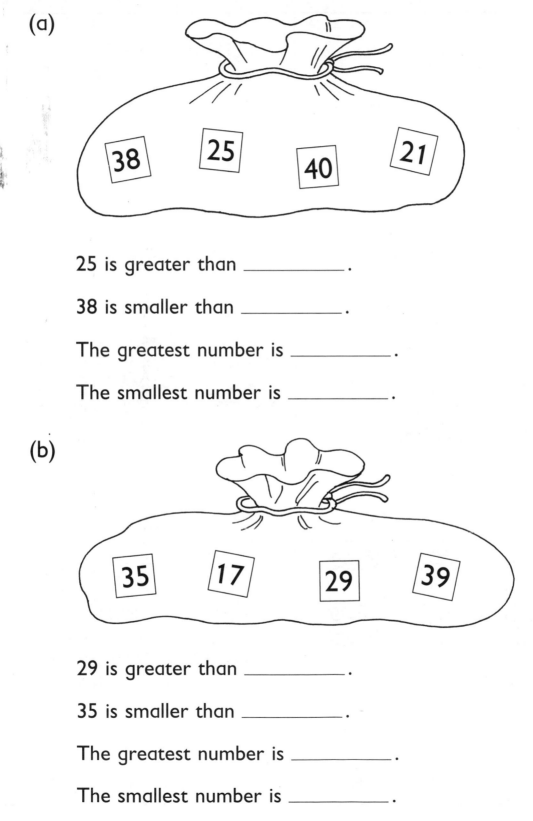

25 is greater than _____ .

38 is smaller than _____ .

The greatest number is _____ .

The smallest number is _____ .

(b)

29 is greater than _____ .

35 is smaller than _____ .

The greatest number is _____ .

The smallest number is _____ .

EXERCISE 16

1. Write how many tens and ones.

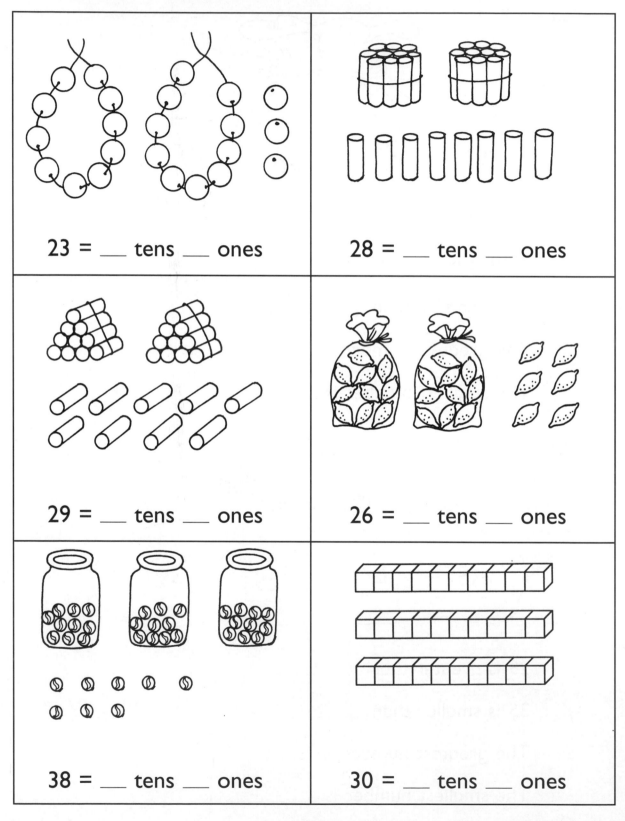

23 = ___ tens ___ ones

28 = ___ tens ___ ones

29 = ___ tens ___ ones

26 = ___ tens ___ ones

38 = ___ tens ___ ones

30 = ___ tens ___ ones

2. Write how many tens and ones. Then write the number.

(a)

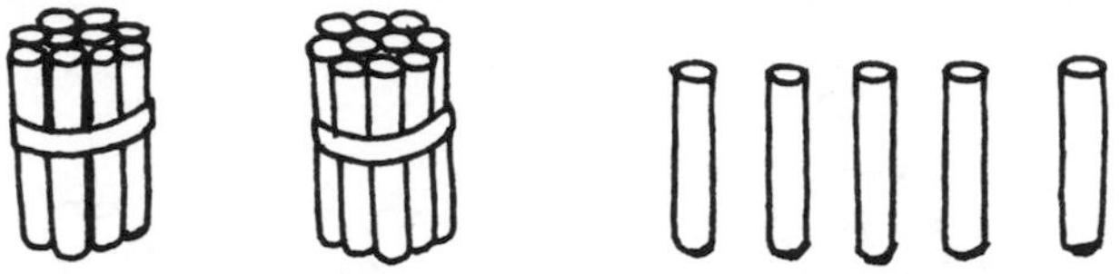

Tens	Ones
2	5

→ 25

(b)

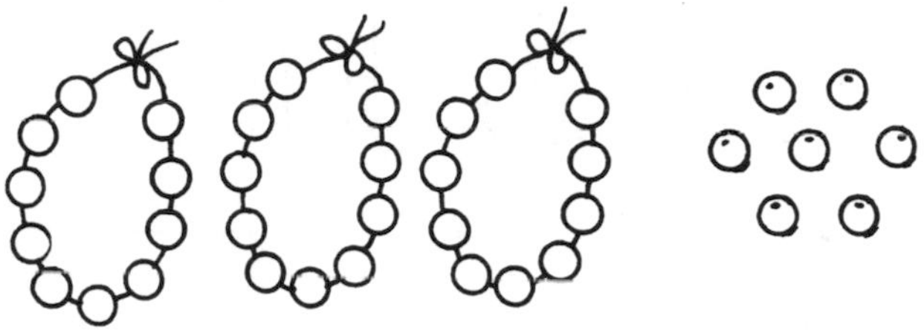

Tens	Ones

→

(c)

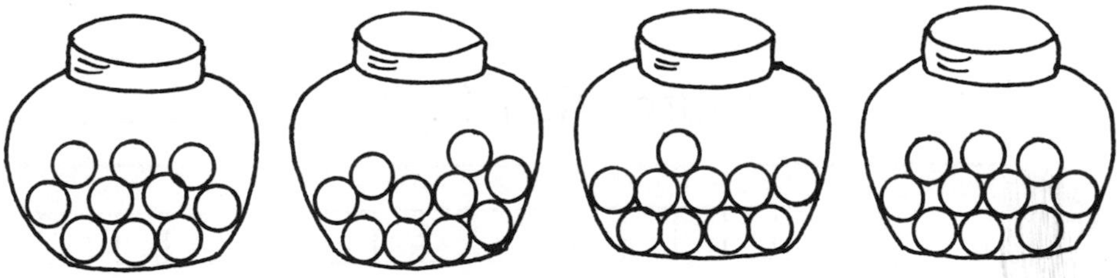

Tens	Ones

→

EXERCISE 17

1. Fill in the blanks.

(a)

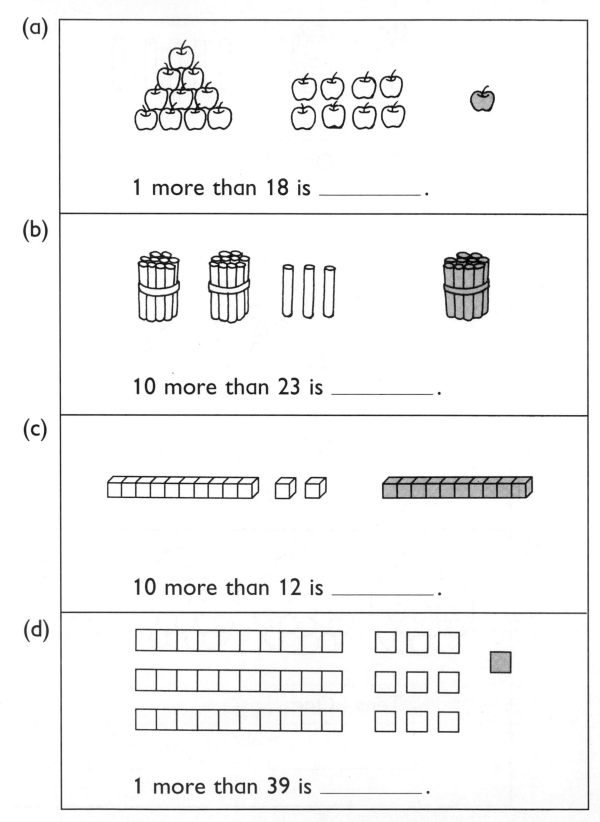

1 more than 18 is _____.

(b)

10 more than 23 is _____.

(c)

10 more than 12 is _____.

(d)

1 more than 39 is _____.

2. Fill in the blanks.

(a)

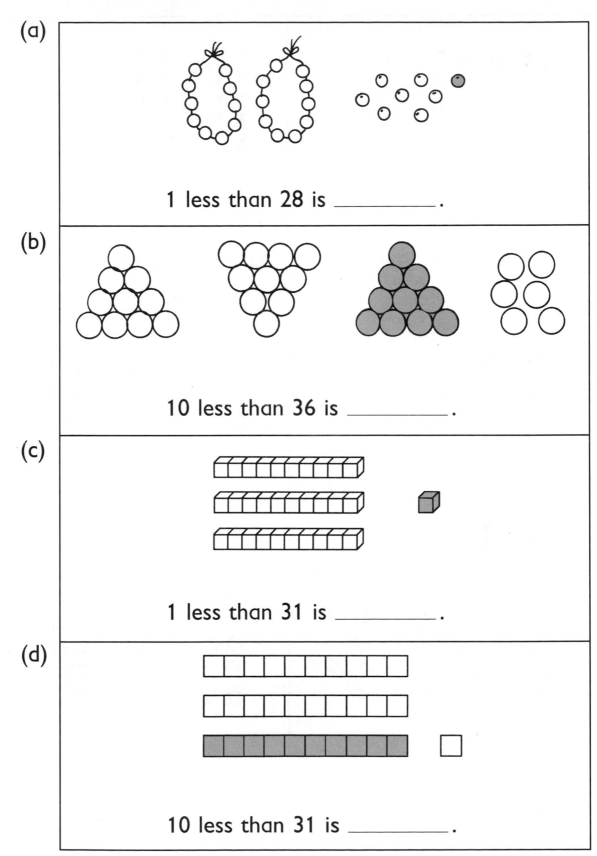

1 less than 28 is _____.

(b)

10 less than 36 is _____.

(c)

1 less than 31 is _____.

(d)

10 less than 31 is _____.

3. Fill in the blanks.

1 more than 25 is _____.

10 more than 25 is _____.

1 less than 22 is _____.

10 less than 22 is _____.

1 more than 24 is _____.

10 more than 24 is _____.

1 more than 27 is _____.

10 more than 27 is _____.

1 less than 26 is _____.

10 less than 26 is _____.

1 less than 29 is _____.

10 less than 29 is _____.

EXERCISE 18

1. Add.

(a)

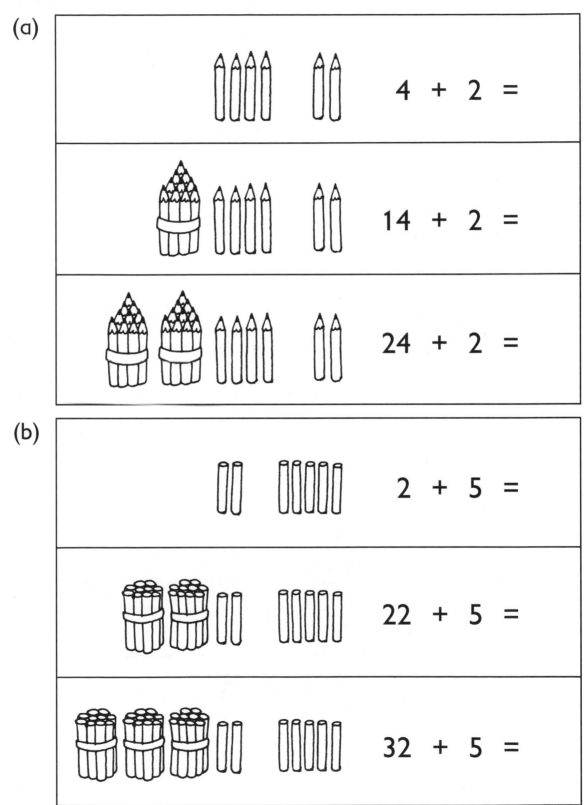

4 + 2 =

14 + 2 =

24 + 2 =

(b)

2 + 5 =

22 + 5 =

32 + 5 =

2. Subtract.

(a)

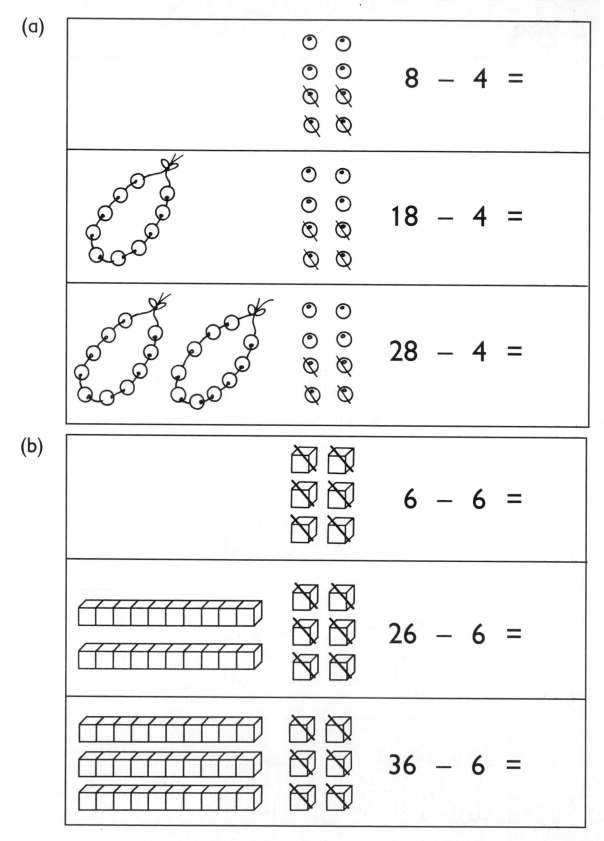

8 – 4 =

18 – 4 =

28 – 4 =

(b)

6 – 6 =

26 – 6 =

36 – 6 =

40

EXERCISE 19

1. Add.

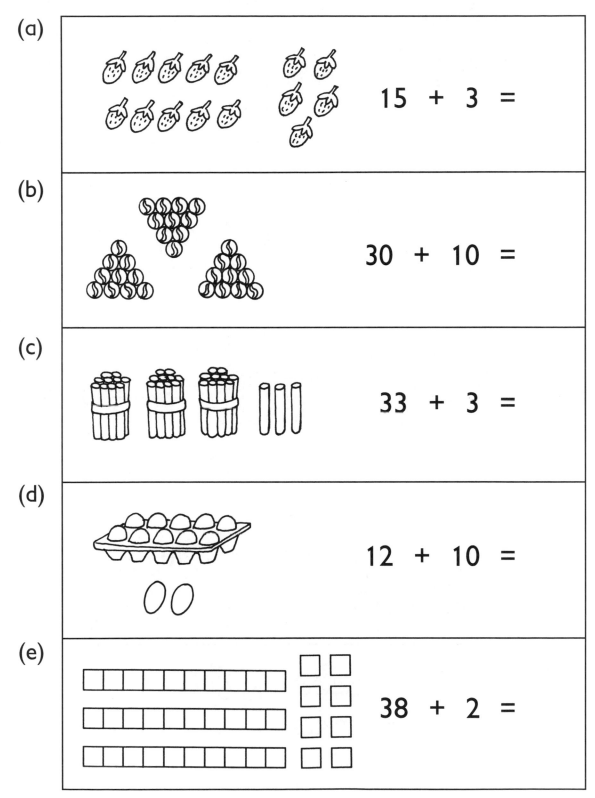

(a) $15 + 3 =$

(b) $30 + 10 =$

(c) $33 + 3 =$

(d) $12 + 10 =$

(e) $38 + 2 =$

2. Subtract.

(a)

$12 - 2 =$

(b)

$25 - 10 =$

(c)

$37 - 3 =$

(d)

$40 - 10 =$

(e)

$36 - 6 =$

EXERCISE 20

1. Write the answers.

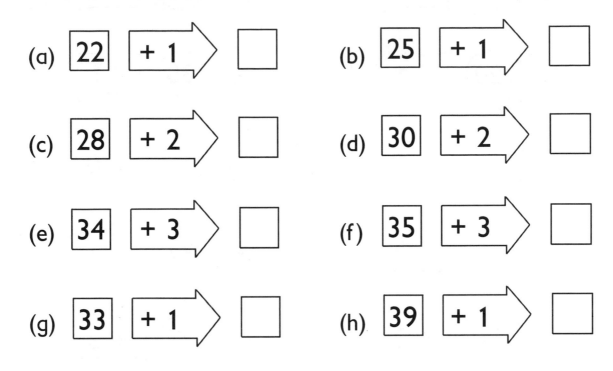

(a) 22 + 1 → ☐   (b) 25 + 1 → ☐

(c) 28 + 2 → ☐   (d) 30 + 2 → ☐

(e) 34 + 3 → ☐   (f) 35 + 3 → ☐

(g) 33 + 1 → ☐   (h) 39 + 1 → ☐

2. Write the answers.

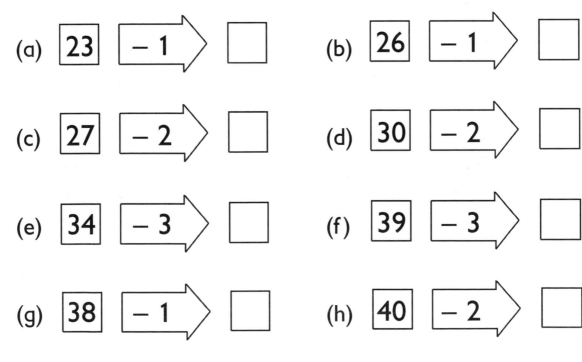

(a) 23 − 1 → ☐   (b) 26 − 1 → ☐

(c) 27 − 2 → ☐   (d) 30 − 2 → ☐

(e) 34 − 3 → ☐   (f) 39 − 3 → ☐

(g) 38 − 1 → ☐   (h) 40 − 2 → ☐

3. Write the answers.

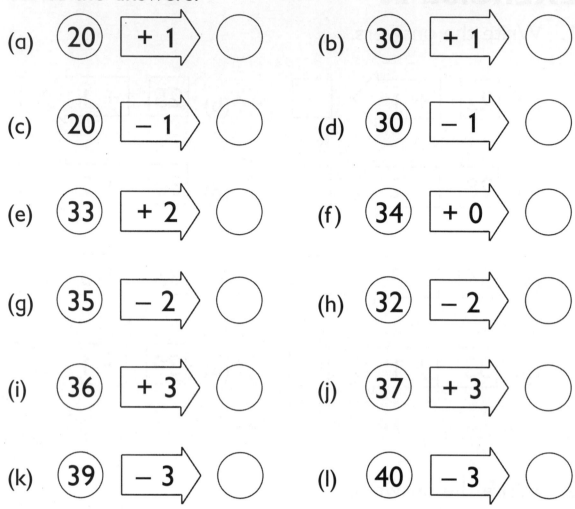

(a) 20 + 1 → ◯

(b) 30 + 1 → ◯

(c) 20 − 1 → ◯

(d) 30 − 1 → ◯

(e) 33 + 2 → ◯

(f) 34 + 0 → ◯

(g) 35 − 2 → ◯

(h) 32 − 2 → ◯

(i) 36 + 3 → ◯

(j) 37 + 3 → ◯

(k) 39 − 3 → ◯

(l) 40 − 3 → ◯

4. Follow the arrows and fill in the missing numbers.

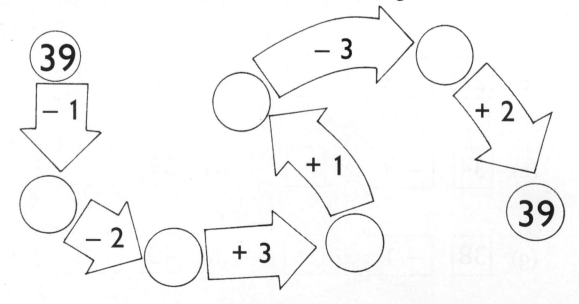

EXERCISE 21

1. Add.

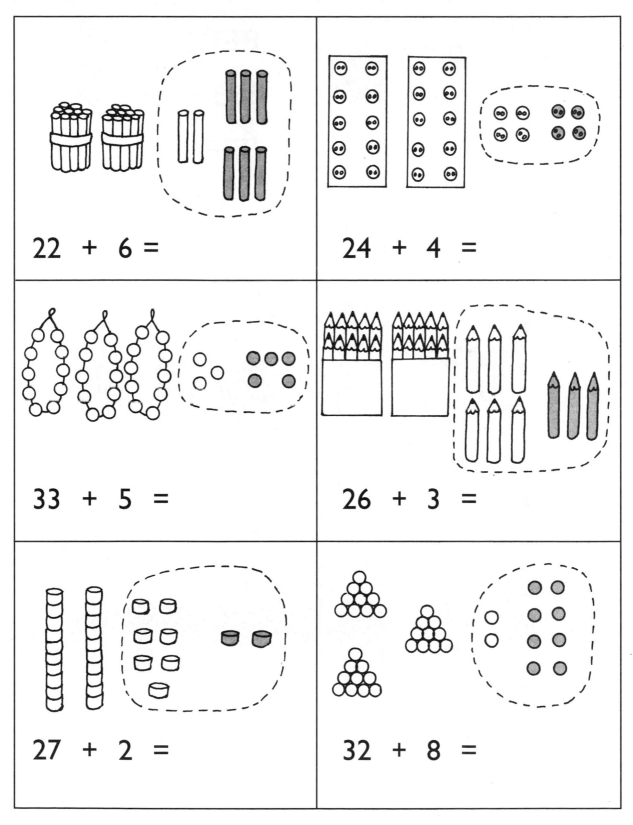

22 + 6 =

24 + 4 =

33 + 5 =

26 + 3 =

27 + 2 =

32 + 8 =

2. Add.

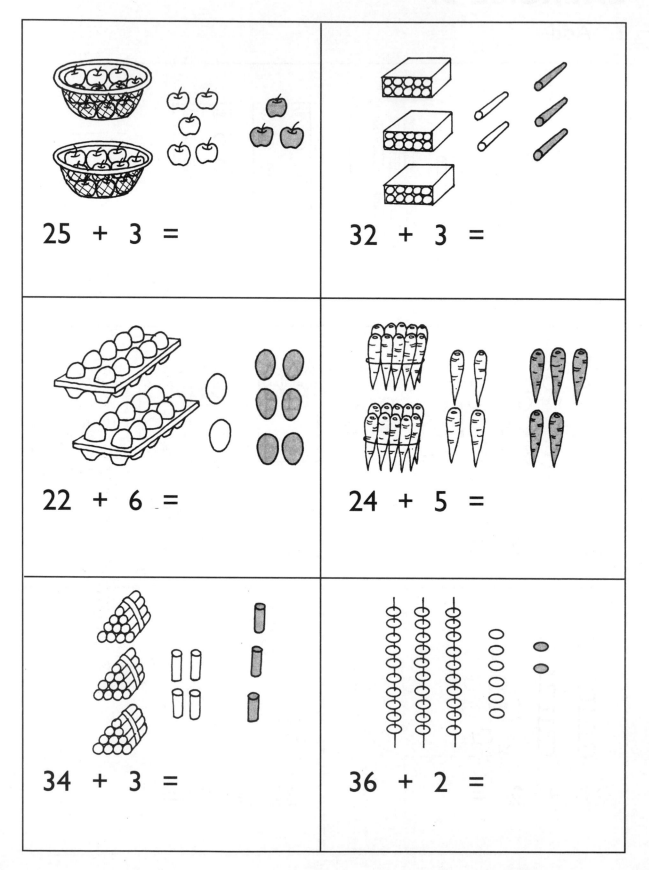

25 + 3 =

32 + 3 =

22 + 6 =

24 + 5 =

34 + 3 =

36 + 2 =

EXERCISE 22

1. Add.

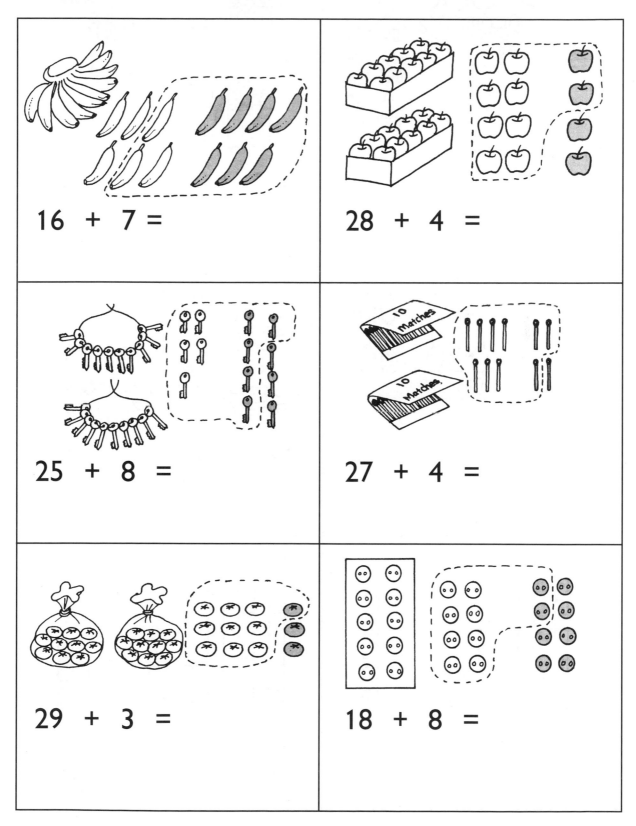

16 + 7 =

28 + 4 =

25 + 8 =

27 + 4 =

29 + 3 =

18 + 8 =

2. Add.

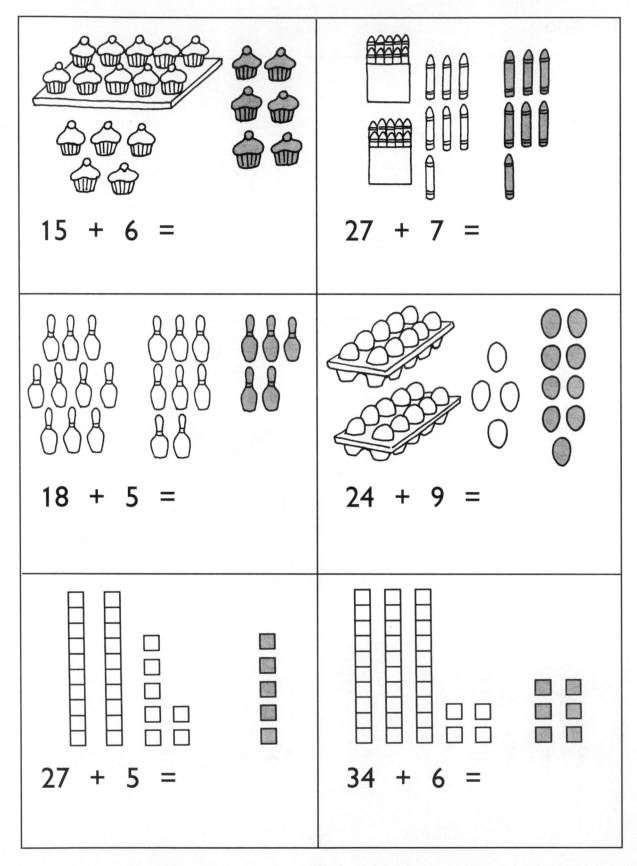

15 + 6 =

27 + 7 =

18 + 5 =

24 + 9 =

27 + 5 =

34 + 6 =

EXERCISE 23

1. Add.

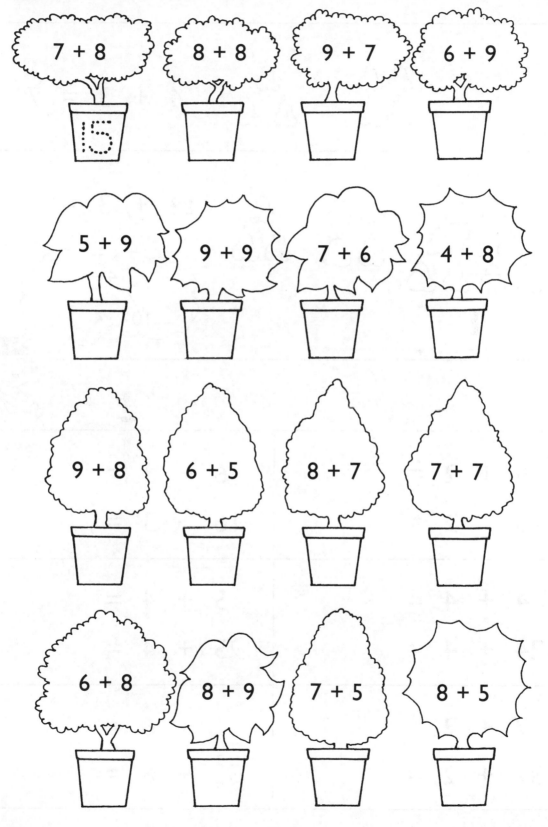

7 + 8   8 + 8   9 + 7   6 + 9

15

5 + 9   9 + 9   7 + 6   4 + 8

9 + 8   6 + 5   8 + 7   7 + 7

6 + 8   8 + 9   7 + 5   8 + 5

EXERCISE 24

1. Add.

$$4 + 3 = 7$$

$$14 + 3 =$$

14 + 3
10   4

$5 + 2 =$ $15 + 2 =$	$6 + 3 =$ $16 + 3 =$
$4 + 4 =$ $24 + 4 =$	$5 + 4 =$ $25 + 4 =$
$7 + 2 =$ $37 + 2 =$	$2 + 6 =$ $32 + 6 =$

2. Add.

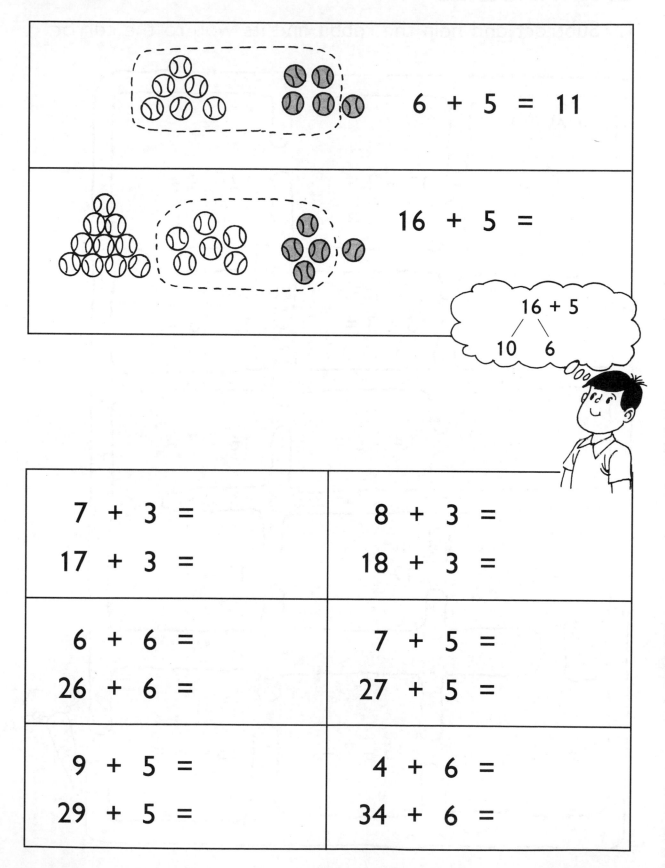

$6 + 5 = 11$

$16 + 5 =$

16 + 5
10   6

$7 + 3 =$ $17 + 3 =$	$8 + 3 =$ $18 + 3 =$
$6 + 6 =$ $26 + 6 =$	$7 + 5 =$ $27 + 5 =$
$9 + 5 =$ $29 + 5 =$	$4 + 6 =$ $34 + 6 =$

EXERCISE 25

1. Subtract and help the rabbit find its way to the carrot.

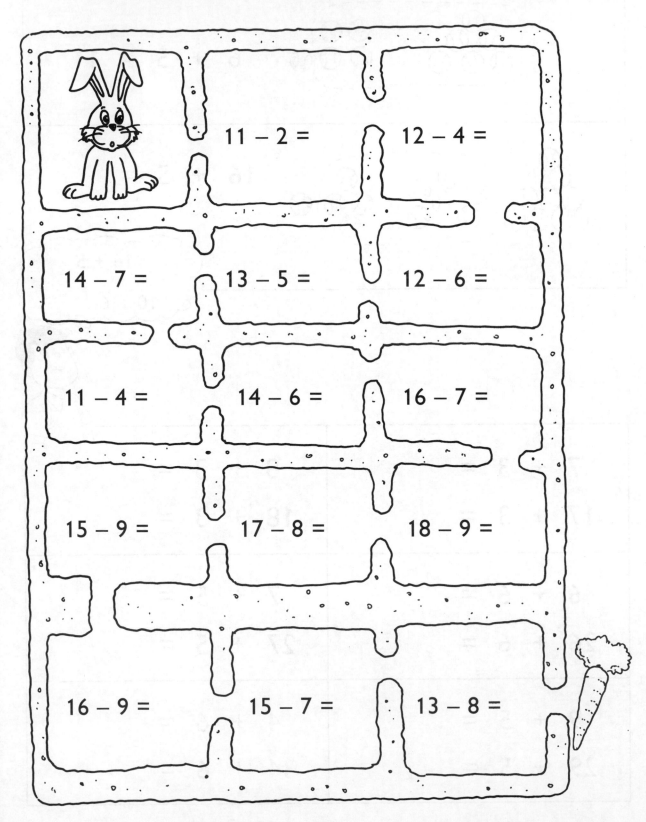

11 − 2 =   12 − 4 =

14 − 7 =   13 − 5 =   12 − 6 =

11 − 4 =   14 − 6 =   16 − 7 =

15 − 9 =   17 − 8 =   18 − 9 =

16 − 9 =   15 − 7 =   13 − 8 =

EXERCISE 26

1. Subtract.

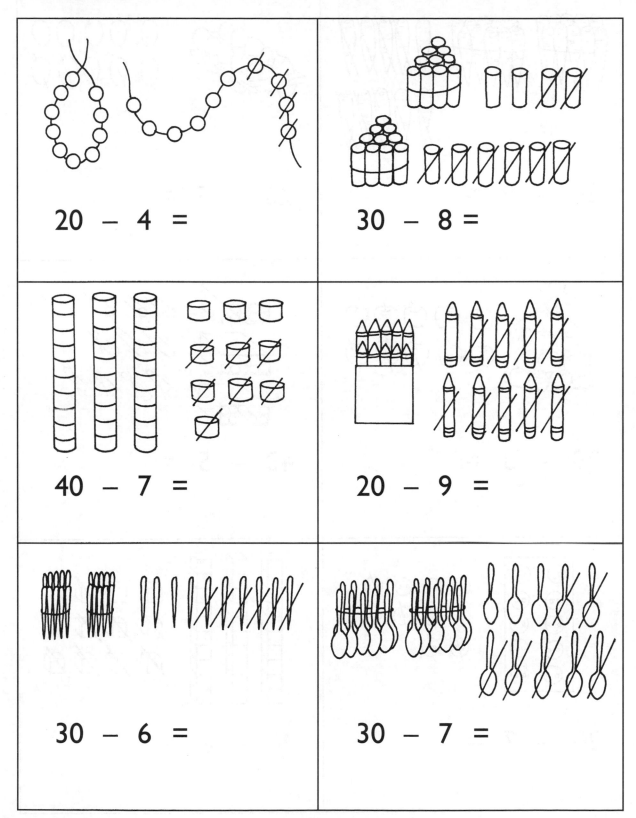

20 – 4 =

30 – 8 =

40 – 7 =

20 – 9 =

30 – 6 =

30 – 7 =

2. Subtract.

30 – 9 =

20 – 5 =

20 – 3 =

40 – 5 =

20 – 7 =

40 – 8 =

EXERCISE 27

1. Subtract.

9 – 6 = 3

29 – 6 =

29 – 6
20   9

8 – 5 =	6 – 4 =
38 – 5 =	26 – 4 =
5 – 3 =	9 – 7 =
25 – 3 =	39 – 7 =
7 – 3 =	8 – 6 =
37 – 3 =	28 – 6 =

2. Subtract.

$12 - 8 = 4$

$22 - 8 =$

$22 - 8$
$10 \quad 12$

$14 - 7 =$ $34 - 7 =$	$15 - 8 =$ $25 - 8 =$
$17 - 9 =$ $27 - 9 =$	$11 - 6 =$ $21 - 6 =$
$13 - 5 =$ $33 - 5 =$	$18 - 9 =$ $38 - 9 =$

EXERCISE 28

1. Add.

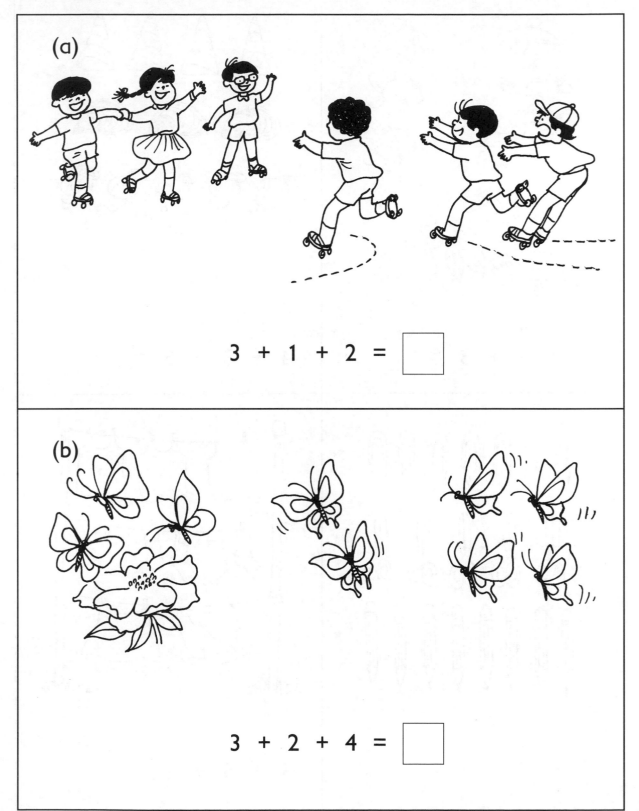

(a)

$$3 + 1 + 2 = \boxed{}$$

(b)

$$3 + 2 + 4 = \boxed{}$$

2. Add.

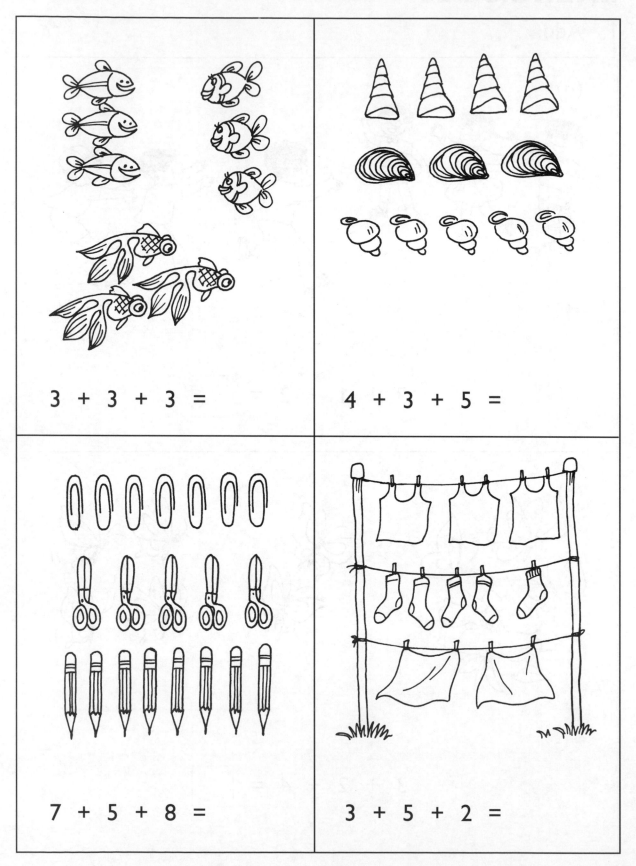

3 + 3 + 3 =

4 + 3 + 5 =

7 + 5 + 8 =

3 + 5 + 2 =

EXERCISE 29

1. Add and write the answers in the circles.

(a)

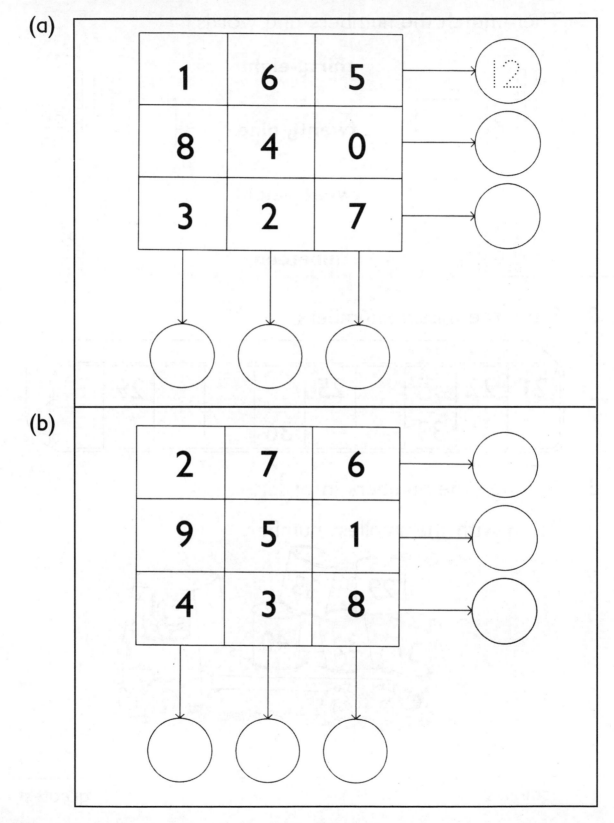

(b)

REVIEW 1

1. Write the numbers.

    Then match the numbers and words.

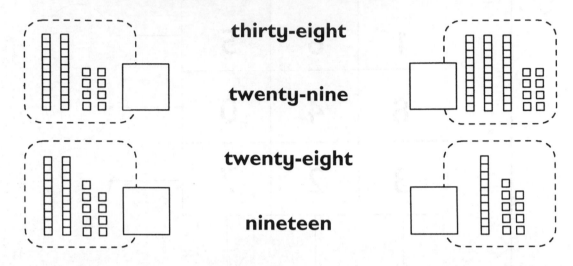

thirty-eight

twenty-nine

twenty-eight

nineteen

2. Fill in the missing numbers.

21	22			25				29	
		33			36				

3. Arrange the numbers in order.

    Begin with the smallest number.

——— , ——— , ——— , ——— , ———

smallest   greatest

4. Fill in the blanks.

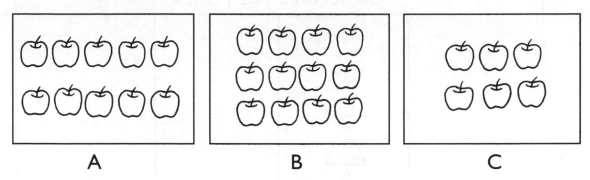

A   B   C

(a)   Set A has _____ more apples than Set C.

(b)   Set A, B and C have _____ apples altogether.

(c)   Set _____ has the most apples.

(d)   Set _____ has the fewest apples.

5. Fill in the missing numbers.

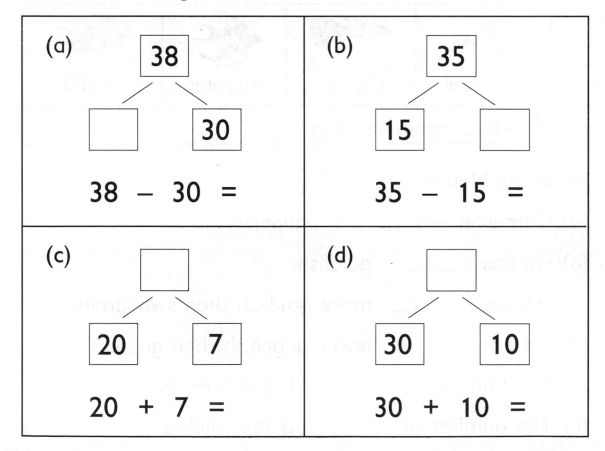

(a)

38

[ ]   30

38 − 30 =

(b)

35

15   [ ]

35 − 15 =

(c)

[ ]

20   7

20 + 7 =

(d)

[ ]

30   10

30 + 10 =

6.

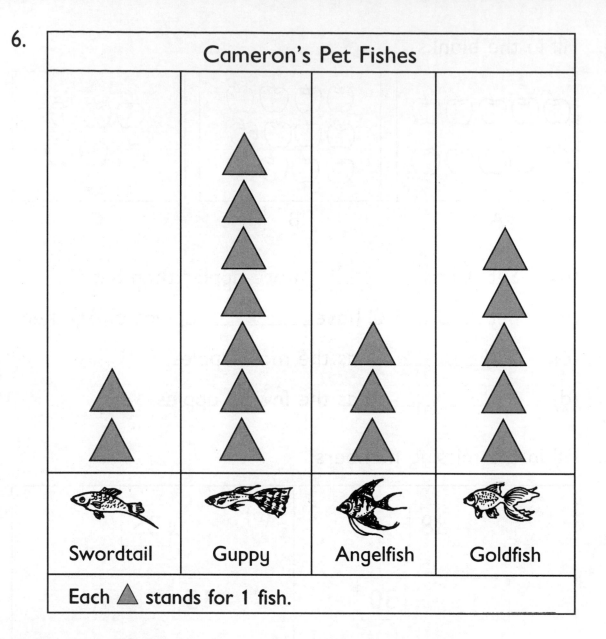

Cameron's Pet Fishes

| Swordtail | Guppy | Angelfish | Goldfish |

Each ▲ stands for 1 fish.

Fill in the blanks.

(a) Cameron has _____ guppies.

(b) He has _____ goldfish.

(c) He has _____ more goldfish than swordtails.

(d) He has _____ fewer angelfish than guppies.

(e) The number of _____ is the greatest.

(f) The number of _____ is the smallest.

7. Mrs. Ray bought 14 pears and 6 oranges.

   How many more pears than oranges were there?

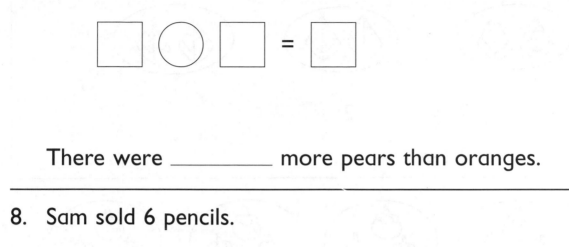

   There were _____ more pears than oranges.

8. Sam sold 6 pencils.

   He had 5 pencils left.

   How many pencils did he have at first?

   Sam had _____ pencils at first.

9. Eric has 8 toy soldiers.

   He buys 7 more.

   How many toy soldiers does he have now?

   He has _____ toy soldiers now.

EXERCISE 30

1. Write the answers.

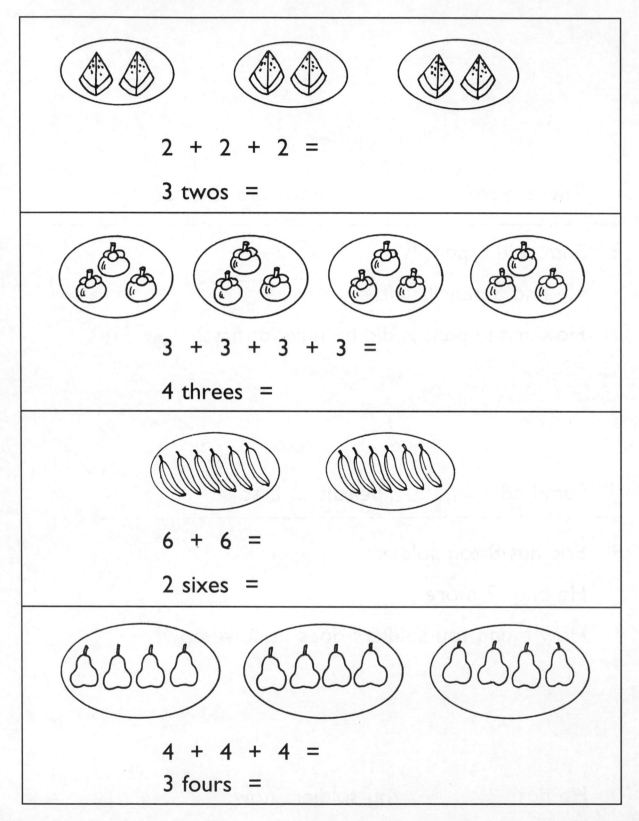

2 + 2 + 2 =

3 twos =

3 + 3 + 3 + 3 =

4 threes =

6 + 6 =

2 sixes =

4 + 4 + 4 =

3 fours =

2. Complete the drawings. Then write the answers.

2 threes =

4 twos =

3 fives =

2 fours =

EXERCISE 31

1. Fill in the blanks.

(a)

There are _____ pencils in each group.

There are _____ pencils altogether.

(b)

There are _____ cakes in each group.

There are _____ cakes altogether.

(c)

There are _____ carrots in each group.

There are _____ carrots altogether.

2. Complete the drawings. Then fill in the blanks.

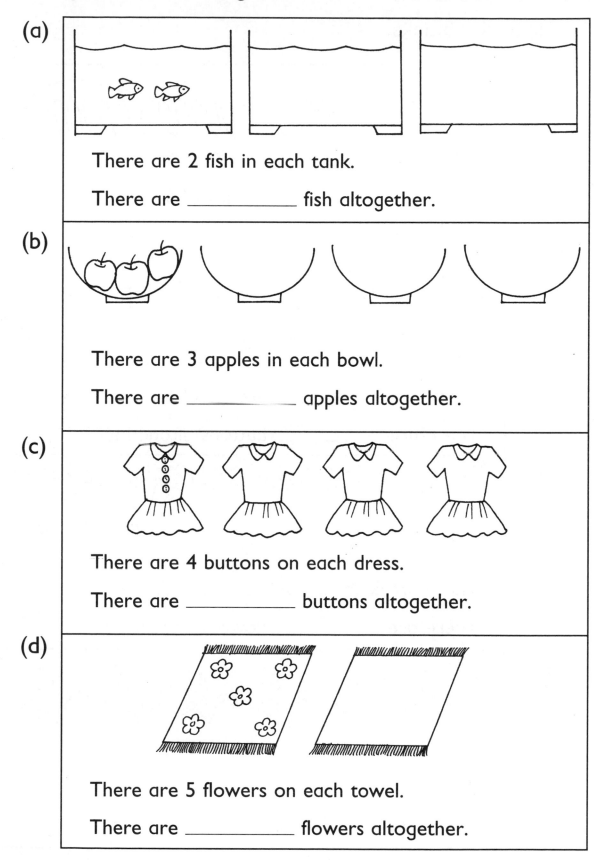

(a) There are 2 fish in each tank.

There are _____ fish altogether.

(b) There are 3 apples in each bowl.

There are _____ apples altogether.

(c) There are 4 buttons on each dress.

There are _____ buttons altogether.

(d) There are 5 flowers on each towel.

There are _____ flowers altogether.

EXERCISE 32

1. Fill in the blanks.

(a)

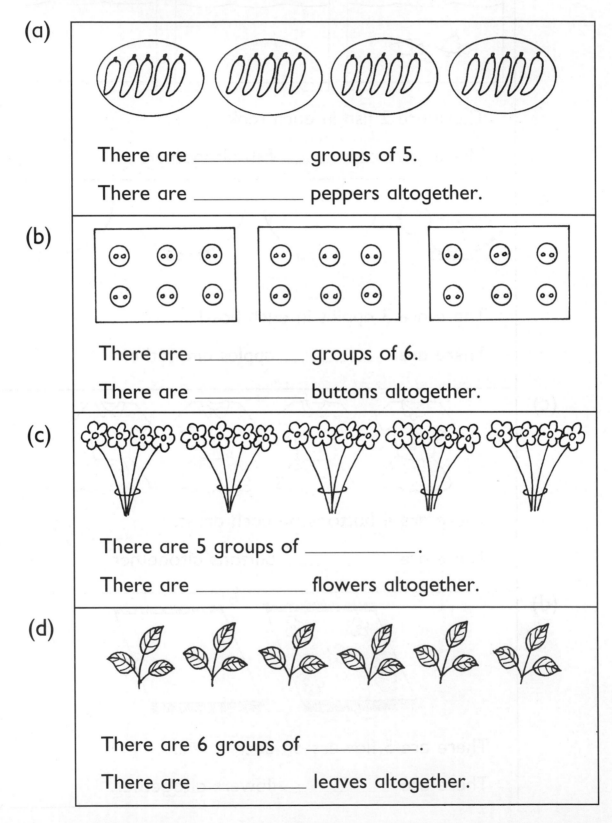

There are _____ groups of 5.

There are _____ peppers altogether.

(b)

There are _____ groups of 6.

There are _____ buttons altogether.

(c)

There are 5 groups of _____ .

There are _____ flowers altogether.

(d)

There are 6 groups of _____ .

There are _____ leaves altogether.

2. (a)

Draw 5 🍎 in each circle.

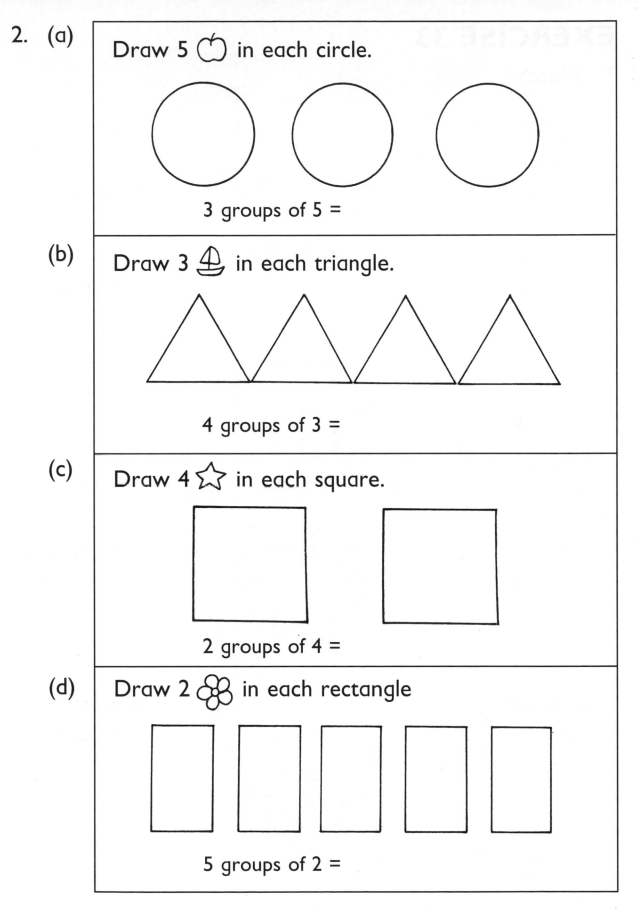

3 groups of 5 =

(b) Draw 3 ⛵ in each triangle.

4 groups of 3 =

(c) Draw 4 ☆ in each square.

2 groups of 4 =

(d) Draw 2 🌸 in each rectangle

5 groups of 2 =

EXERCISE 33

1. Match.

5 fours

3 eights

3 groups of 8

5 groups of 4

5 × 4

Multiply 5 and 4

Multiply 3 and 8

3 × 8

Multiply 6 and 3

Multiply 4 and 10

6 × 3

4 tens

6 threes

6 groups of 3

4 groups of 10

4 × 10

2. Tell a story for each picture.

   Then complete the number sentence.

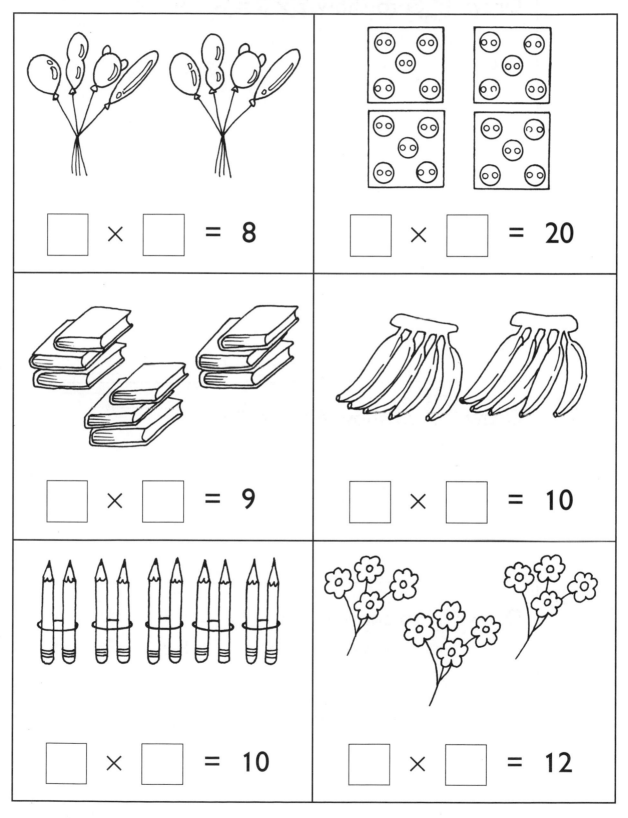

$\boxed{} \times \boxed{} = 8$

$\boxed{} \times \boxed{} = 20$

$\boxed{} \times \boxed{} = 9$

$\boxed{} \times \boxed{} = 10$

$\boxed{} \times \boxed{} = 10$

$\boxed{} \times \boxed{} = 12$

EXERCISE 34

1. (a)

Draw 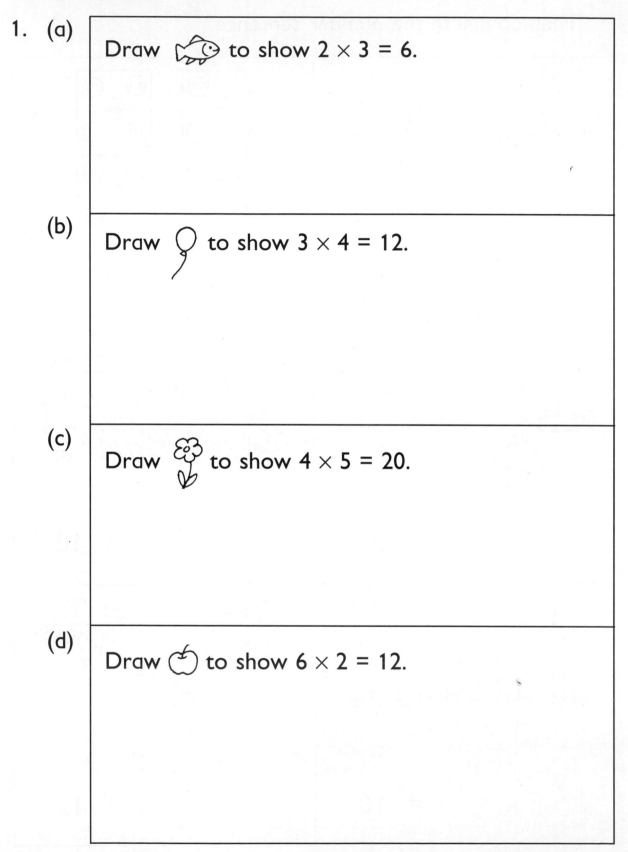 to show 2 × 3 = 6.

(b)

Draw to show 3 × 4 = 12.

(c)

Draw to show 4 × 5 = 20.

(d)

Draw to show 6 × 2 = 12.

EXERCISE 35

1. Match and write the answers.

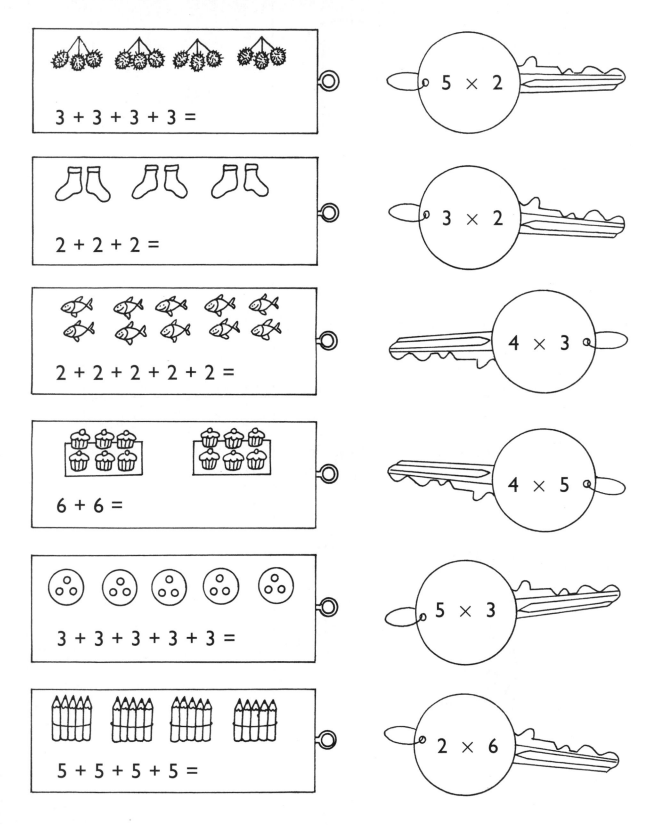

3 + 3 + 3 + 3 =

5 × 2

2 + 2 + 2 =

3 × 2

2 + 2 + 2 + 2 + 2 =

4 × 3

6 + 6 =

4 × 5

3 + 3 + 3 + 3 + 3 =

5 × 3

5 + 5 + 5 + 5 =

2 × 6

2. Write the answers.

(a)

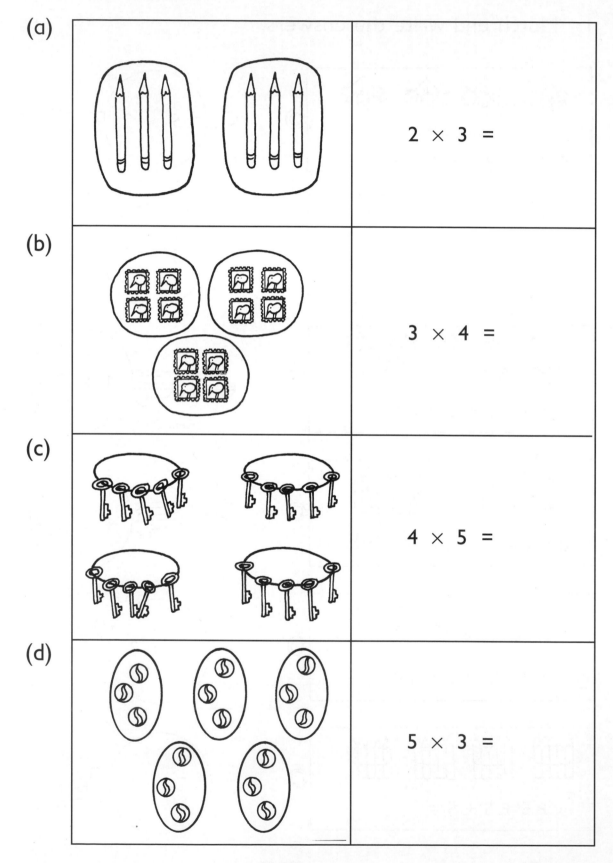

$2 \times 3 =$

(b)

$3 \times 4 =$

(c)

$4 \times 5 =$

(d)

$5 \times 3 =$

3. Multiply.

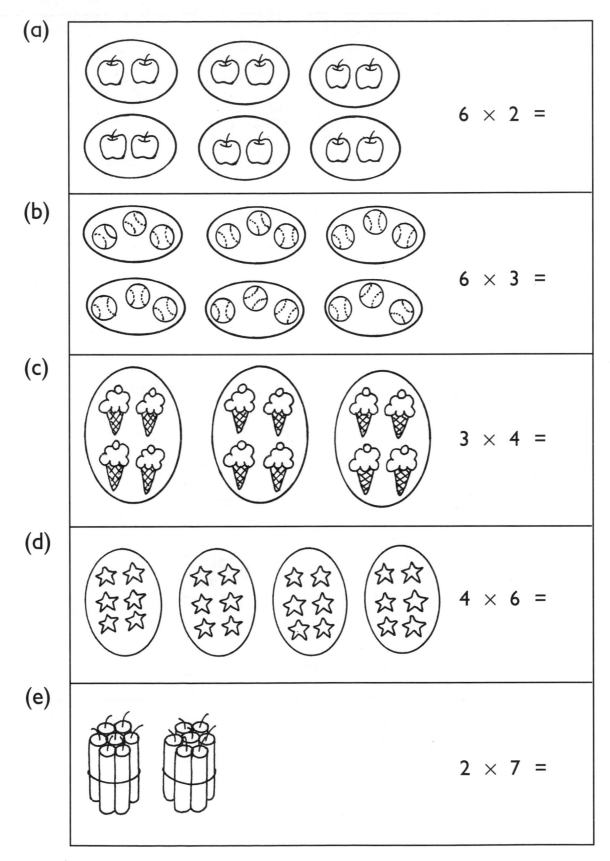

(a) $6 \times 2 =$

(b) $6 \times 3 =$

(c) $3 \times 4 =$

(d) $4 \times 6 =$

(e) $2 \times 7 =$

EXERCISE 36

1.

How many apples are there altogether?

☐ ◯ ☐ = ☐

There are _____ apples altogether.

2.

How many fish are there altogether?

☐ ◯ ☐ = ☐

There are _____ fish altogether.

3.

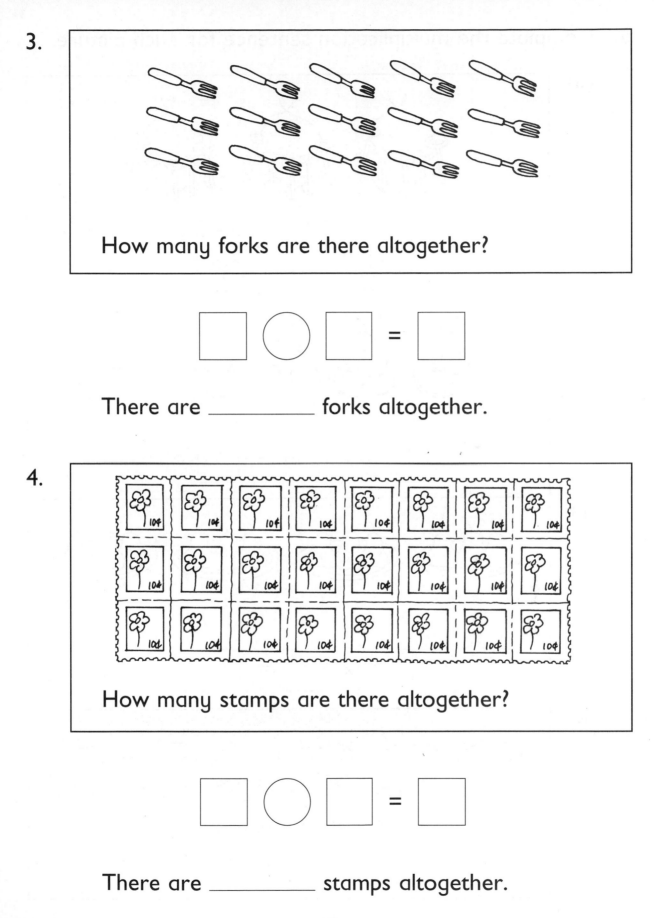

How many forks are there altogether?

□ ○ □ = □

There are _____ forks altogether.

4.

How many stamps are there altogether?

□ ○ □ = □

There are _____ stamps altogether.

5. Complete the multiplication sentence for each picture.

(a)

☐ × ☐ = ☐

(b)

☐ × ☐ = ☐

(c)

☐ × ☐ = ☐

(d)

☐ × ☐ = ☐

REVIEW 2

1. Write the numbers.

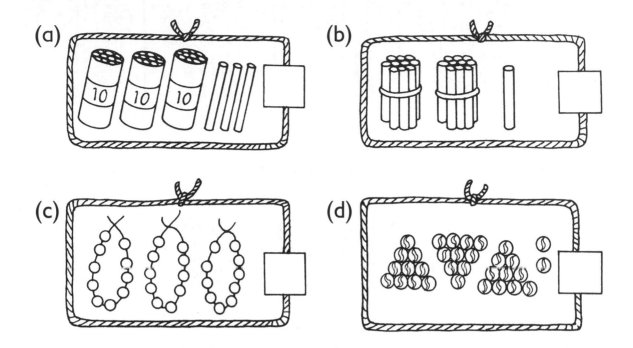

(a)   (b)   (c)   (d)

2. David has 4 marbles.

   Pablo has 2 more marbles than David.

   Draw Pablo's marbles.

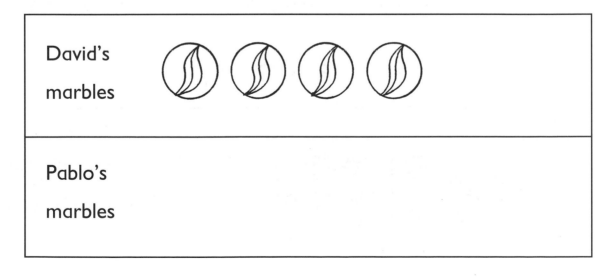

| David's marbles | |
| Pablo's marbles | |

Pablo has _____ marbles.

3. Multiply.

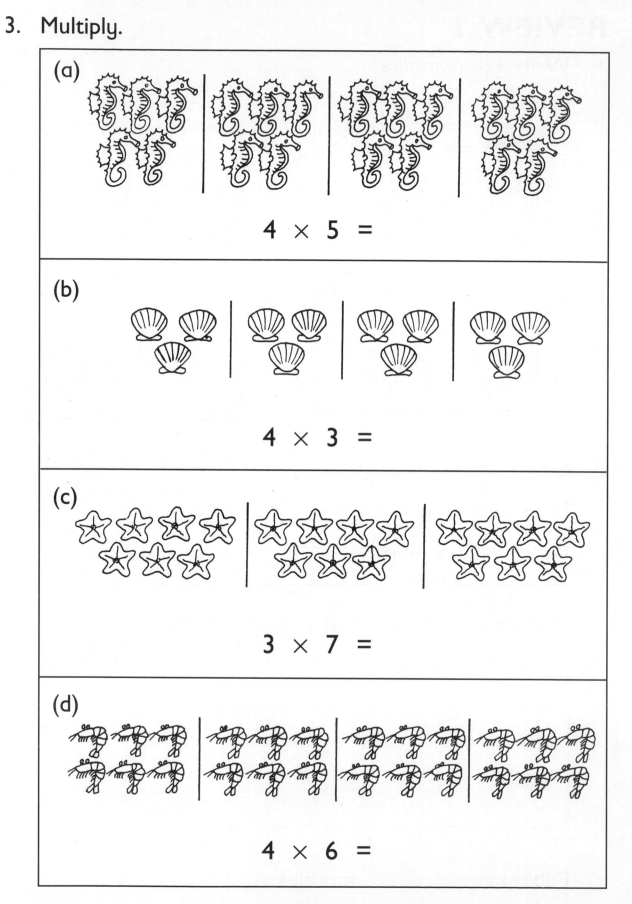

(a)

$4 \times 5 =$

(b)

$4 \times 3 =$

(c)

$3 \times 7 =$

(d)

$4 \times 6 =$

4. Fill in the blanks.

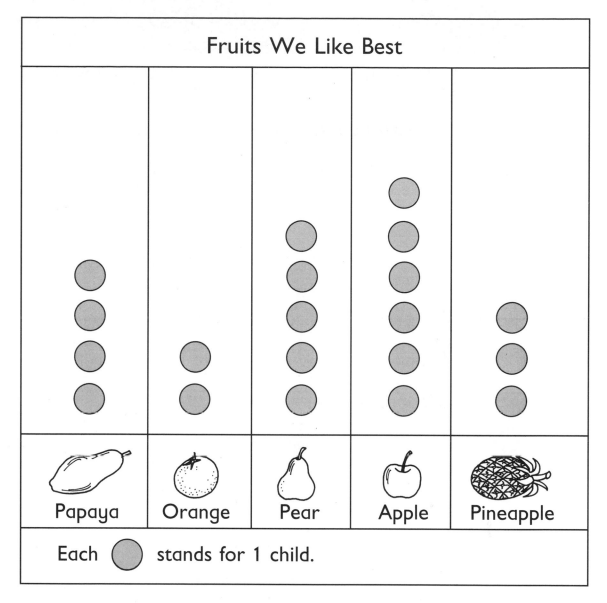

Fruits We Like Best

Each ⬤ stands for 1 child.

(a) There are _____ children altogether.

(b) _____ children like to eat papayas.

(c) The most popular fruit is _____.

(d) The least popular fruit is _____.

(e) _____ more children like pears than pineapples.

(f) _____ fewer children like oranges than apples.

5.

Emily's

Lily's flowers

How many more flowers does Lily have than Emily?

☐ ◯ ☐ = ☐

Lily has _____ more flowers than Emily.

6. Holly has 5 cartons of orange juice.

She buys 7 more.

How many cartons does she have now?

She has _____ cartons now.

7. Sara picks 17 shells.

She throws away 5.

How many shells does she have left?

She has _____ shells left.

REVIEW 3

1. Do these.

(a)
$$4 + 6 =$$
$$14 + 6 =$$
$$24 + 6 =$$
$$34 + 6 =$$

(b)
$$10 - 7 =$$
$$20 - 7 =$$
$$30 - 7 =$$
$$40 - 7 =$$

(c)
$$8 + 10 =$$
$$8 + 20 =$$
$$8 + 30 =$$

(d)
$$39 - 10 =$$
$$39 - 20 =$$
$$39 - 30 =$$

2. Fill in the blanks.

(a)

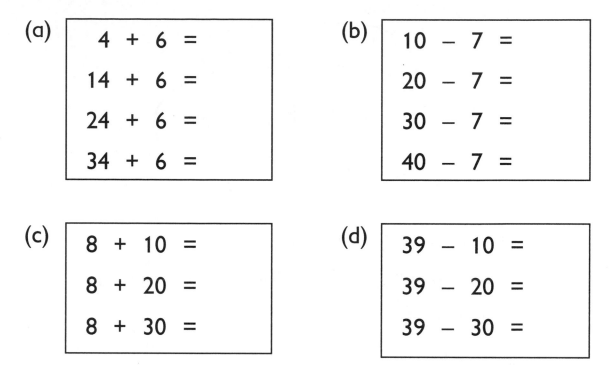

_____ has more marbles.

He has _____ more marbles.

(b)

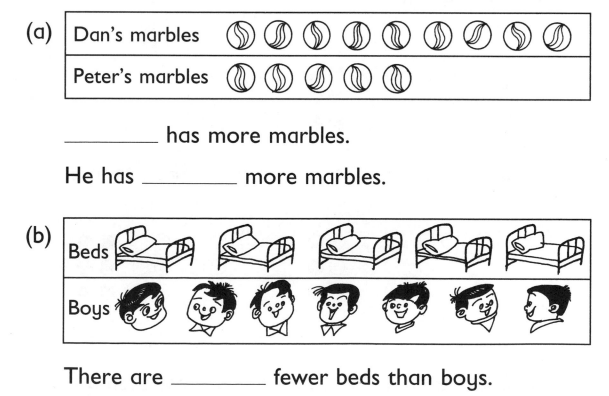

There are _____ fewer beds than boys.

83

3. (a) Circle the greatest number.

   (b) Cross out the smallest number.

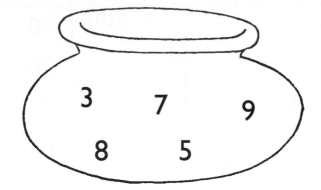

4. Fill in the missing numbers.

   (a) 25, 26, _____, _____, 29, _____, _____, 32

   (b) 2, 4, 6, 8, _____, _____, _____, _____

   (c) 5, 10, 15, _____, _____, 30, _____, _____

5. Fill in the blanks.

   (a)

   6 more than 30 is ___.

   (b)

   10 more than 22 is ___.

   (c)

   2 less than 40 is ___.

   (d)

   10 less than 36 is ___.

84

6. Complete the number sentences.

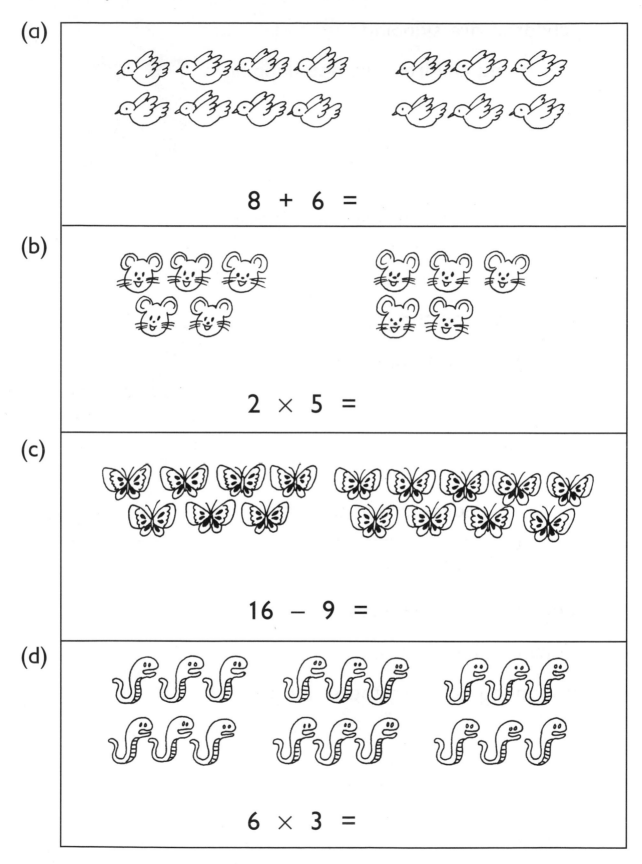

(a)

8 + 6 =

(b)

2 × 5 =

(c)

16 − 9 =

(d)

6 × 3 =

7. There are 19 children.

    6 children are skipping.

    How many children are not skipping?

    _____ children are not skipping.

8. There are 9 cakes altogether.

    4 cakes are on the plate.

    How many cakes are in the box?

    _____ cakes are in the box.

9. There are 5 blue cars.

    There are 4 yellow cars.

    There are 2 red cars.

    How many cars are there altogether?

    There are _____ cars altogether.

REVIEW 4

1. (a) Add or subtract.

20 + 14 = 34 − 20 = 34 − 14 = 14 + 20 =	

(b) Multiply.

3 × 5 =	

2. Draw two lines to divide the square below into a rectangle and two triangles.

3. (a) Color the 3rd ball from the right.

   (b) Cross out the 5th ball from the left.

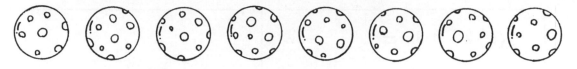

4. Fill in the blanks.

   (a) 1 more than 7 is _____.

   (b) 1 less than 7 is _____.

5. Arrange the ribbons, A, B, C and D in order. Begin with the shortest ribbon.

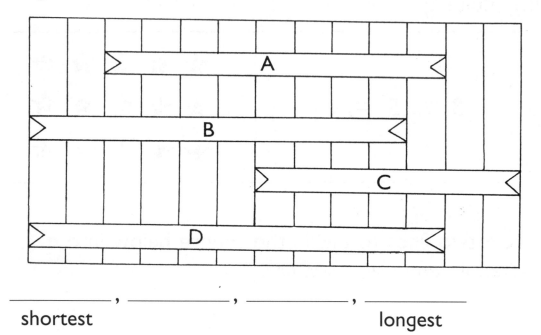

   _____ , _____ , _____ , _____
   shortest   longest

6. Check (✓) the heavier fruit

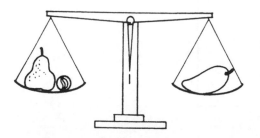

Mango 🥭	
Pear 🍐	

7.

How many fish are there altogether?

$$3 \times 4 =$$

There are _____ fish altogether.

8.

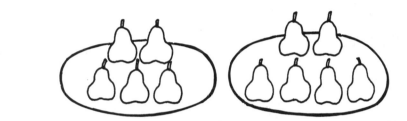

How many pears are there altogether?

$$5 + 6 =$$

There are _____ pears altogether.

---

9. How many more ducks than chickens are there?

$$9 - 6 =$$

There are _____ more ducks than chickens.

10. Ryan caught **11** butterflies.

    David caught **9** butterflies.

    How many more butterflies did Ryan catch than David?

    Ryan caught _____ more butterflies than David.

---

11. Amy has **8** lanterns.

    She gives away **5** lanterns.

    How many lanterns does she have left?

    Amy has _____ lanterns left.

---

12. Mary wants **12** buttons for her dress.

    She has **8** buttons now.

    How many more buttons does she need?

    She needs _____ more buttons.

EXERCISE 37

1. Fill in the blanks.

(a)

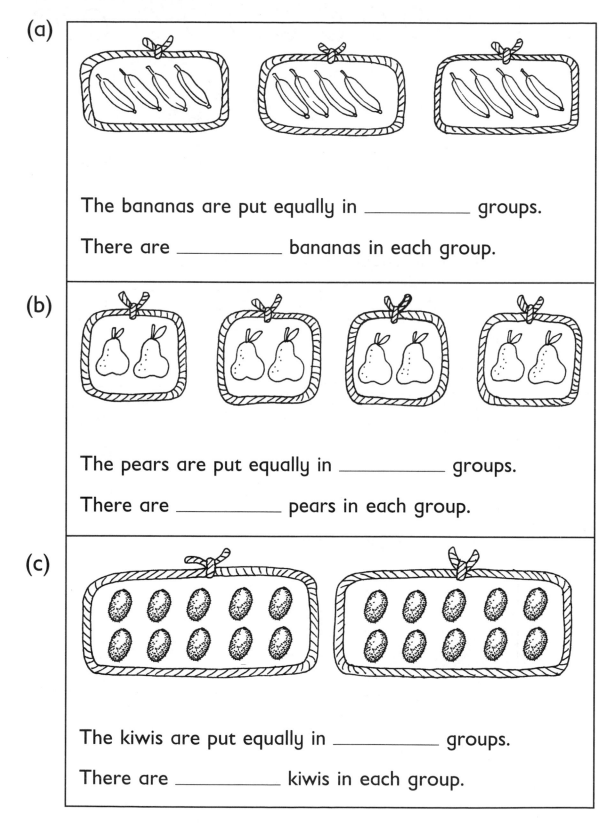

The bananas are put equally in _____ groups.

There are _____ bananas in each group.

(b)

The pears are put equally in _____ groups.

There are _____ pears in each group.

(c)

The kiwis are put equally in _____ groups.

There are _____ kiwis in each group.

2. (a)

Draw an equal number of eggs for each nest.

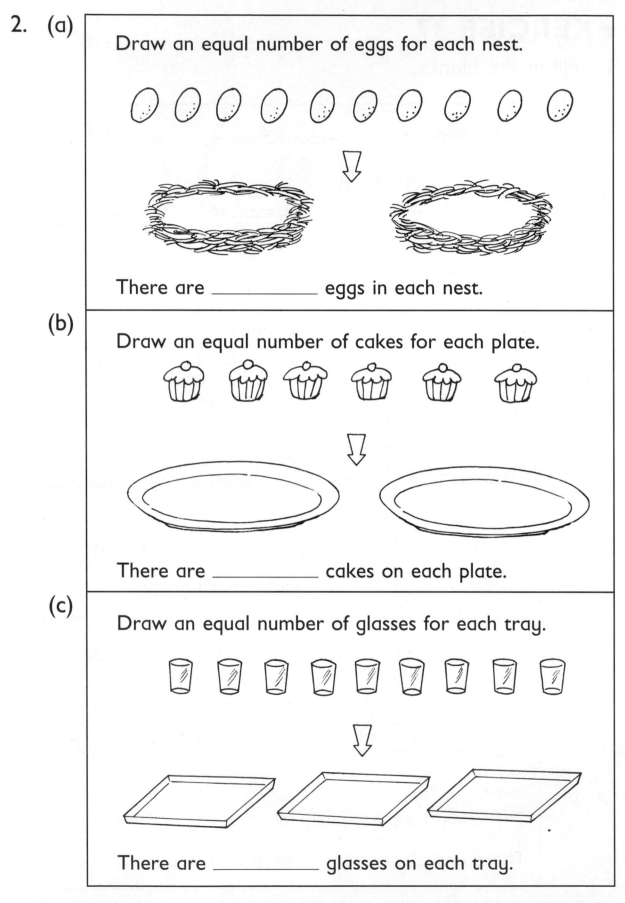

There are _____ eggs in each nest.

(b)

Draw an equal number of cakes for each plate.

There are _____ cakes on each plate.

(c)

Draw an equal number of glasses for each tray.

There are _____ glasses on each tray.

EXERCISE 38

1.

Put 18 pears equally in 3 groups.

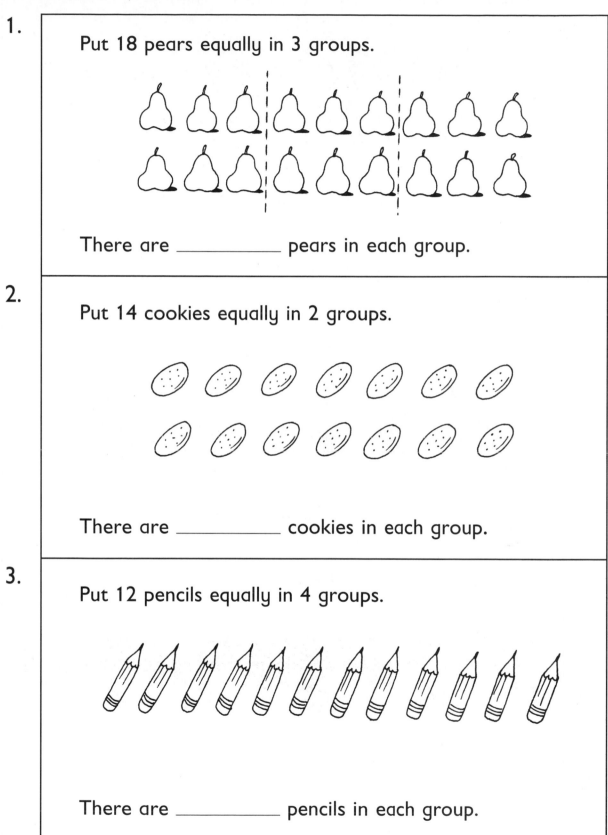

There are _____ pears in each group.

2.

Put 14 cookies equally in 2 groups.

There are _____ cookies in each group.

3.

Put 12 pencils equally in 4 groups.

There are _____ pencils in each group.

4.

Put 16 pencils equally in 2 groups.

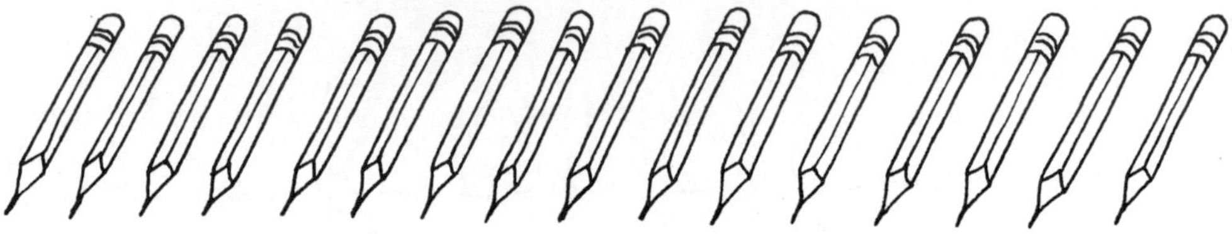

There are _____ pencils in each group.

5.

Put 12 flowers equally in 3 groups.

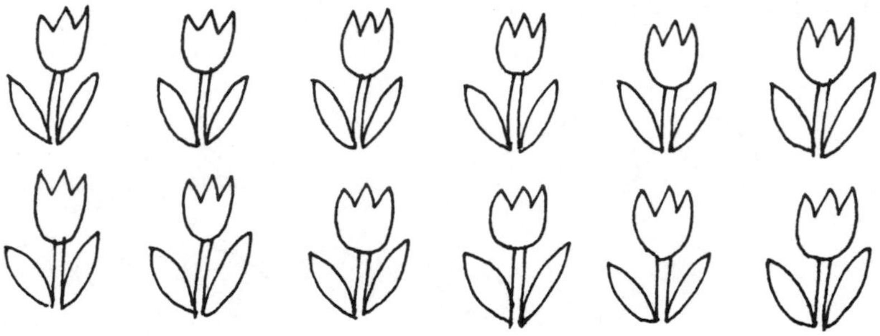

There are _____ flowers in each group.

6.

Put 15 fish equally in 3 groups.

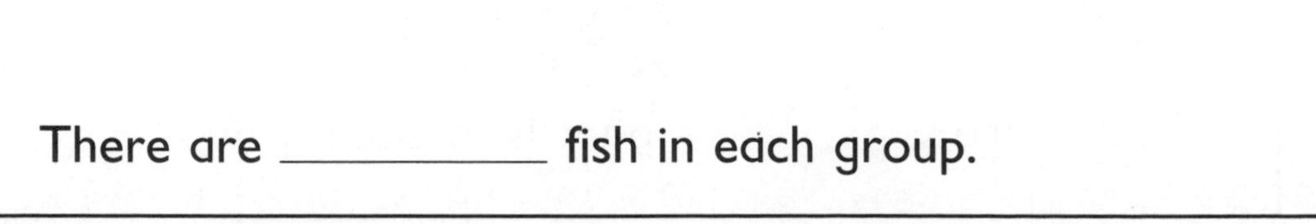

There are _____ fish in each group.

EXERCISE 39

1. (a)

There are 10 children.

Circle groups of 2.

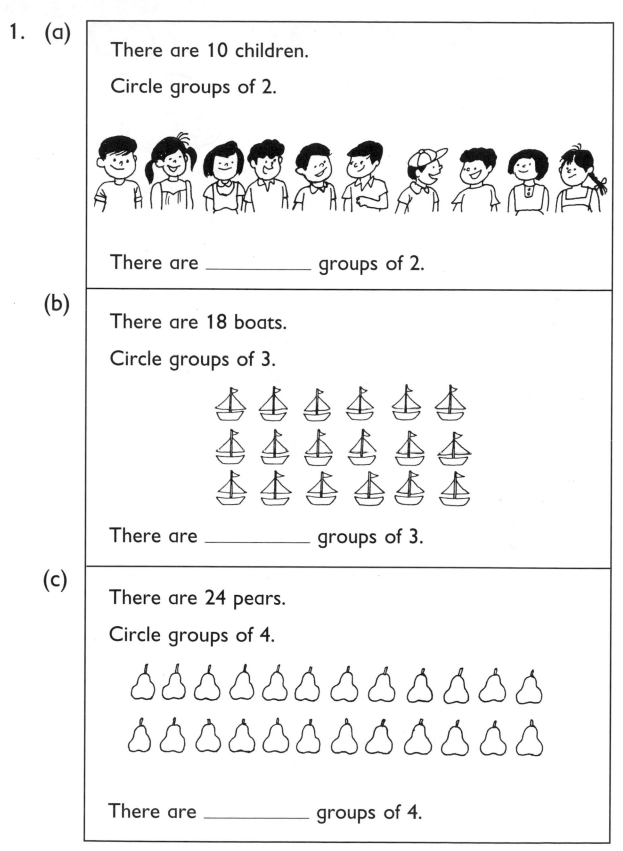

There are _____ groups of 2.

(b)

There are 18 boats.

Circle groups of 3.

There are _____ groups of 3.

(c)

There are 24 pears.

Circle groups of 4.

There are _____ groups of 4.

2. (a)

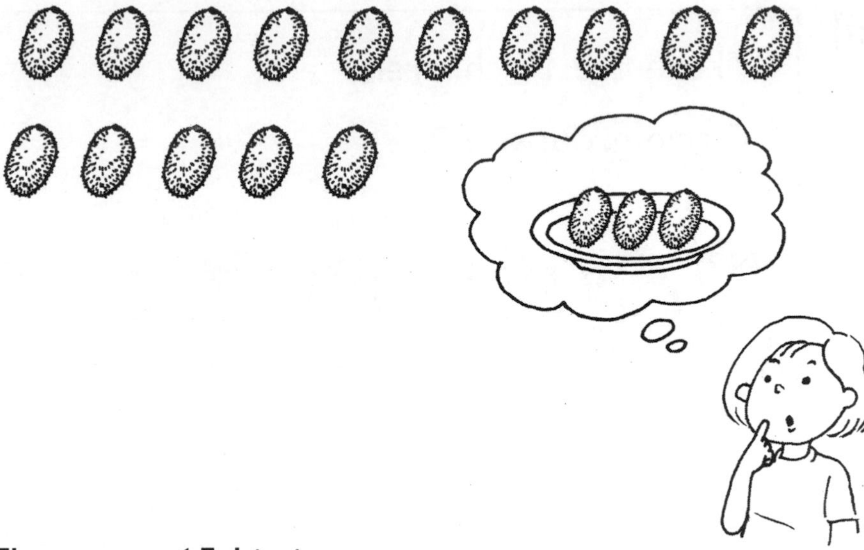

There are 15 kiwis.

Kate puts 3 kiwis on each plate.

She uses _____ plates.

(b)

Lily has 18 beads.

She puts 3 beads on each string.

She uses _____ strings.

EXERCISE 40

1.

2 girls share 10 beads equally.

How many beads does each girl get?

Each girl gets _____ beads.

2.

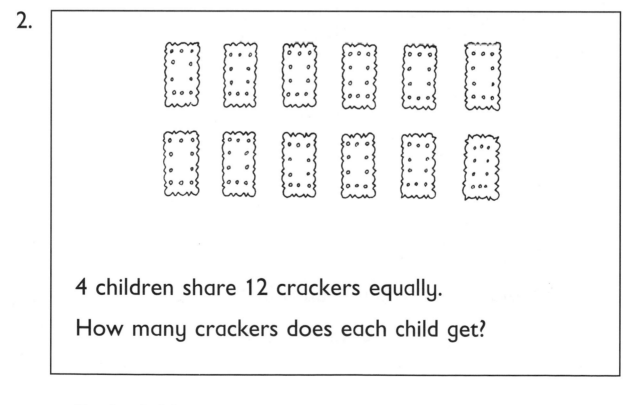

4 children share 12 crackers equally.

How many crackers does each child get?

Each child gets _____ crackers.

3.

Divide 12 picture cards into 3 equal groups.

How many picture cards are there in each group?

There are _____ picture cards in each group.

4.

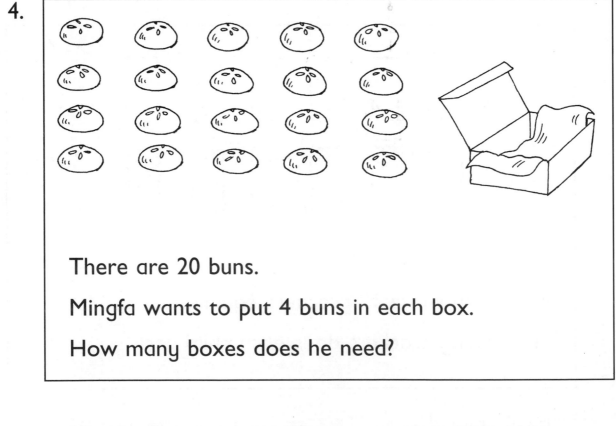

There are 20 buns.

Mingfa wants to put 4 buns in each box.

How many boxes does he need?

He needs _____ boxes.

EXERCISE 41

1. Write Yes or No.

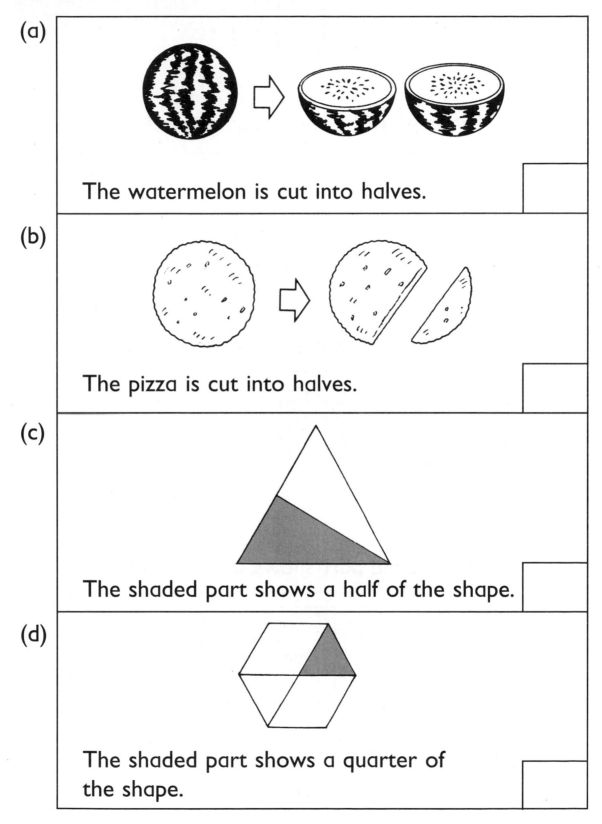

(a) The watermelon is cut into halves.

(b) The pizza is cut into halves.

(c) The shaded part shows a half of the shape.

(d) The shaded part shows a quarter of the shape.

(e)

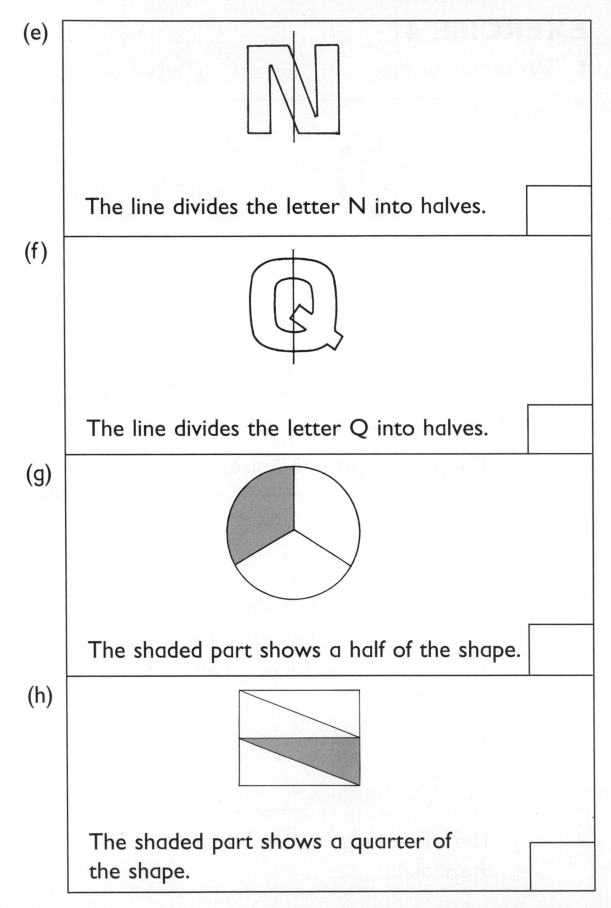

The line divides the letter N into halves.

(f)

The line divides the letter Q into halves.

(g)

The shaded part shows a half of the shape.

(h)

The shaded part shows a quarter of the shape.

EXERCISE 42

1. Color a half of each of the following shapes.

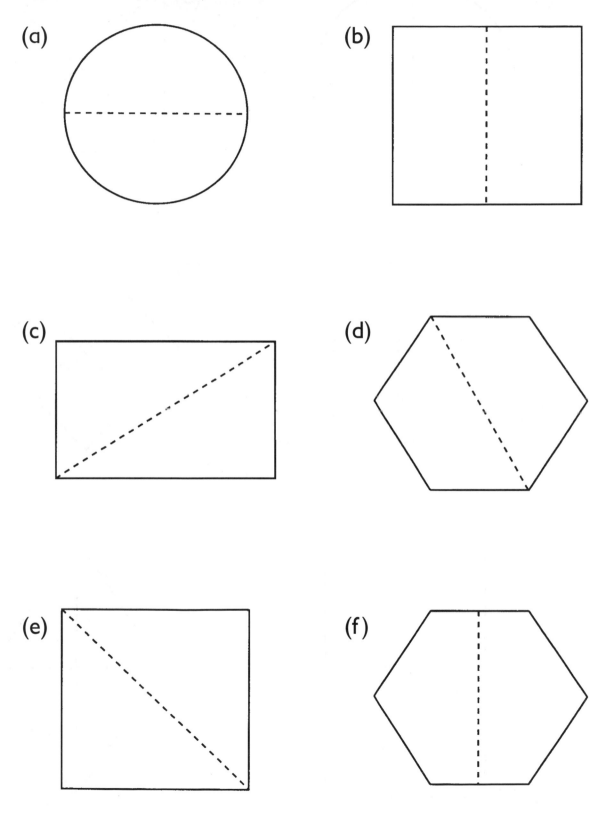

(a)

(b)

(c)

(d)

(e)

(f)

2. Color a quarter of each of the following shapes.

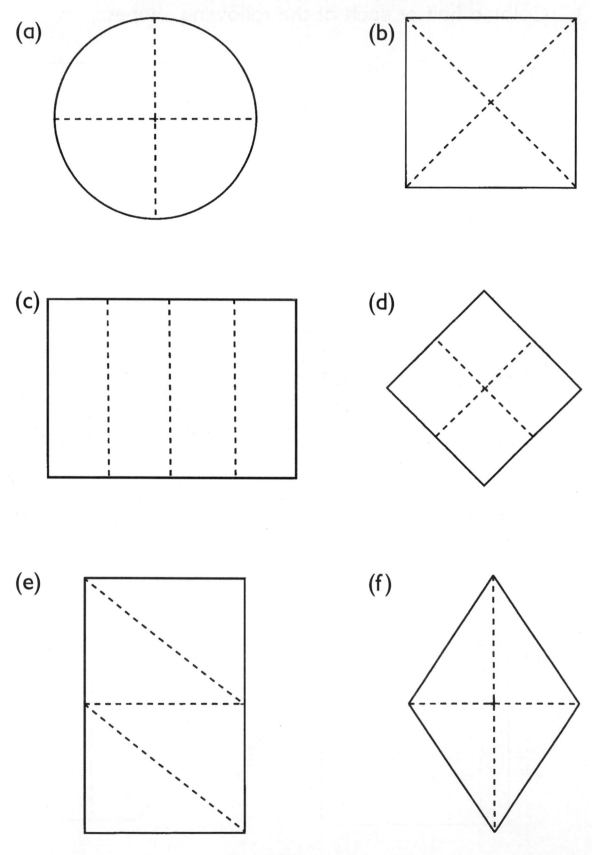

(a)

(b)

(c)

(d)

(e)

(f)

EXERCISE 43

1. Color the last shape to continue the pattern.

(a)

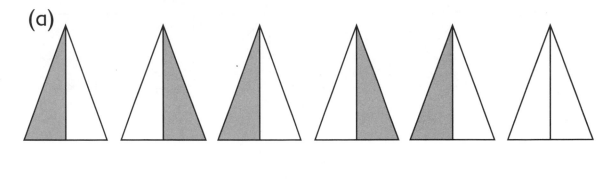

(b)

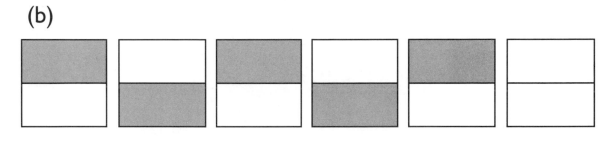

(c)

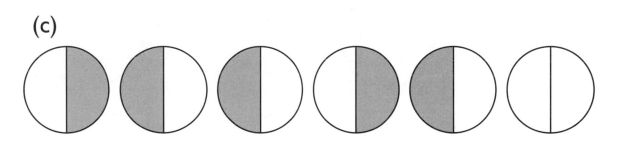

(d)

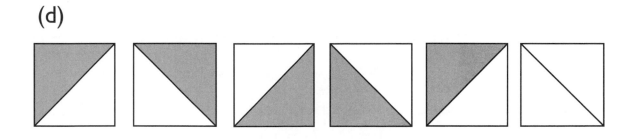

(e)

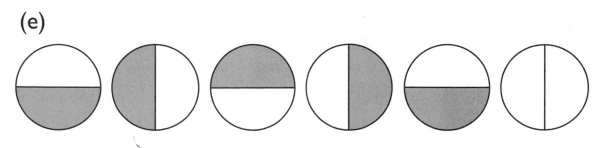

2. Color the last shape to continue the pattern.

(a)

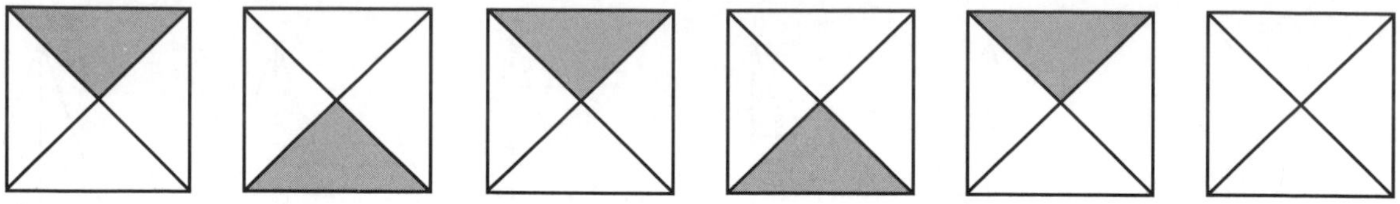

(b)

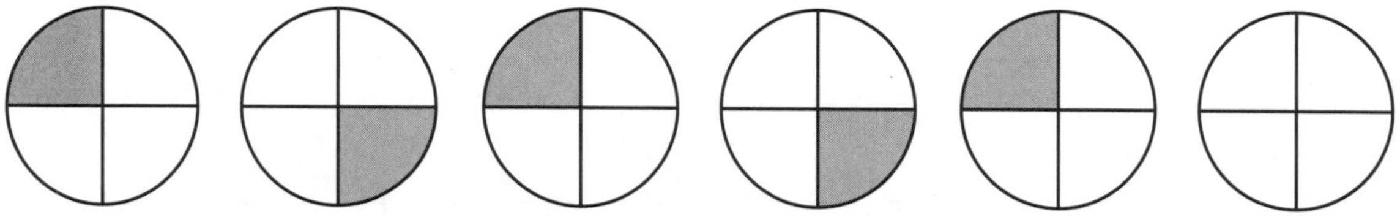

(c)

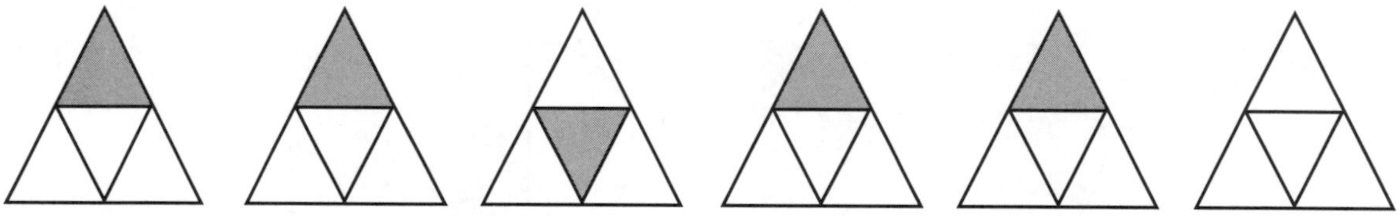

(d)

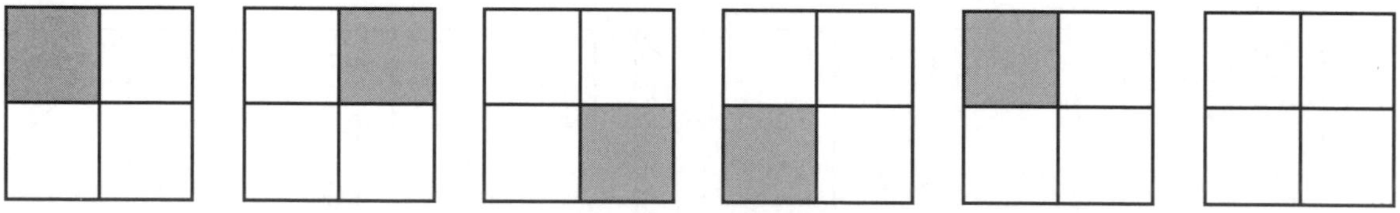

(e)

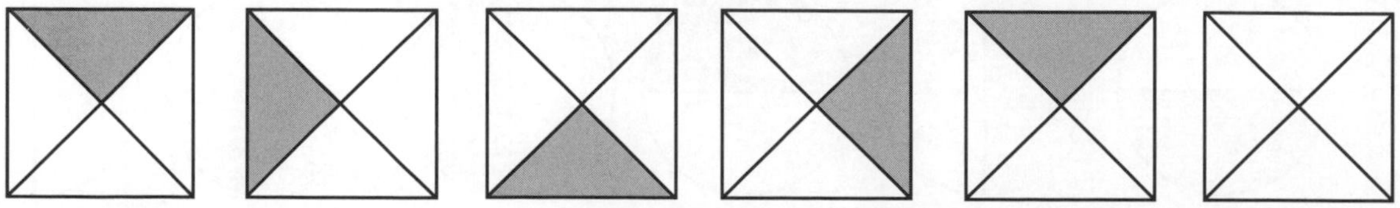

EXERCISE 44

1. Match.

8 o'clock

5 o'clock

1 o'clock

3 o'clock

11 o'clock

10 o'clock

7 o'clock

9 o'clock

2. Write the time shown on each clock.

(a)

Matthew has lunch at _____.

(b)

He does his homework at _____.

(c)

He goes swimming at _____.

(d)

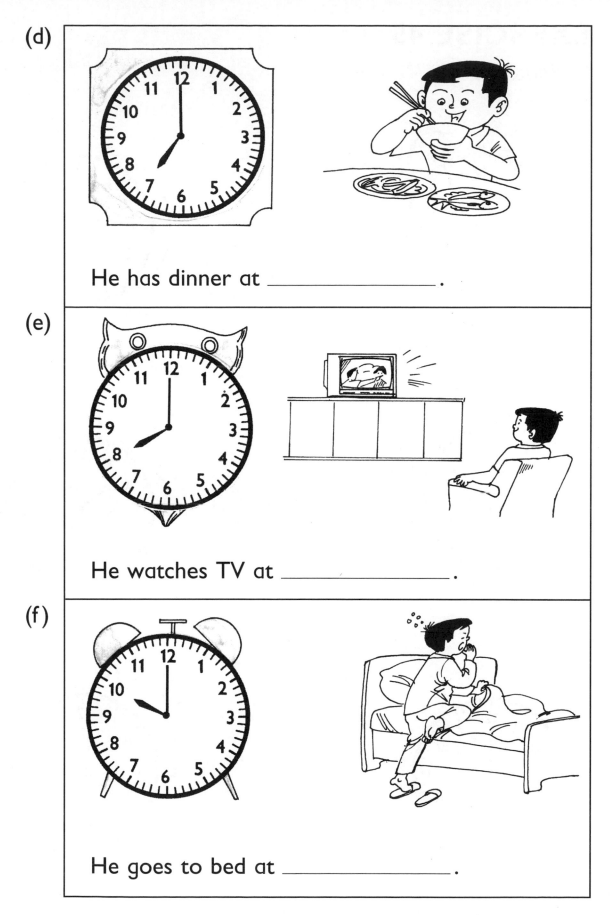

He has dinner at _____ .

(e)

He watches TV at _____ .

(f)

He goes to bed at _____ .

EXERCISE 45

1. Match.

half past 6

half past 2

6 o'clock

half past 7

half past 10

5 o'clock

2. Write the time shown on each clock face.

Arrival:

_____

At the
Butterfly Park:

_____

At Fort Siloso:

_____

At the
Underwater
World:

_____

3. Write the time shown on each clock.

_____   _____

_____   _____

_____   _____

REVIEW 5

1. Write the numbers.

    (a)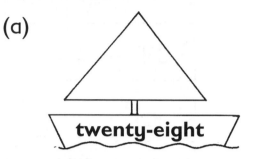

    (b)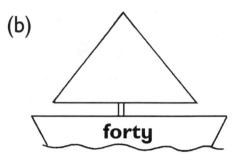

2. Fill in the missing numbers.

    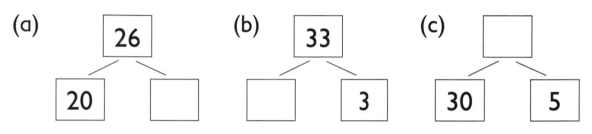

    (a)

    (b)

    (c)

3. Fill in the missing numbers.

    5, 10, _____, 20, _____, _____, _____, 40

4. Fill in the missing numbers.

    (a) 5 more than 10 is ☐.

    (b) 10 more than 10 is ☐.

    (c) 4 less than 24 is ☐.

    (d) 10 less than 38 is ☐.

111

5. Add or subtract.

   Then pair up the number sentences.

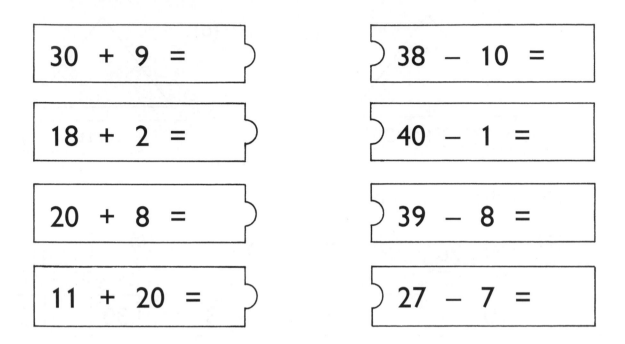

30 + 9 =   38 – 10 =

18 + 2 =   40 – 1 =

20 + 8 =   39 – 8 =

11 + 20 =   27 – 7 =

6. Match.

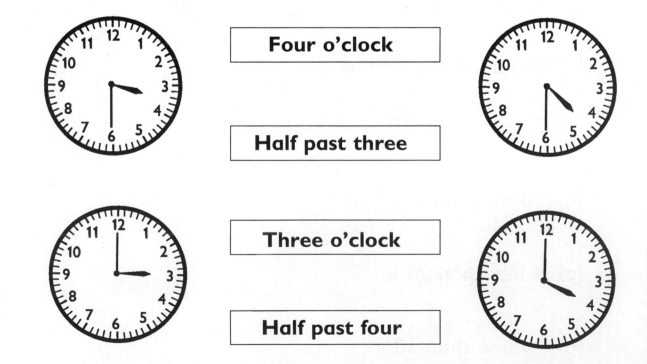

Four o'clock

Half past three

Three o'clock

Half past four

7.

I have 6 stamps.

I have 4 stamps.

I have 5 stamps.

David

Tyrone

Ryan

How many stamps do they have altogether?

☐ ○ ☐ ○ ☐ = ☐

They have _____ stamps altogether.

8.

I have 12 books.

I have 3 more books than Amber.

Amber

Lily

How many books does Lily have?

☐ ○ ☐ = ☐

Lily has _____ books.

9. Emma bought 14 apples.

   She gave 10 apples to her friends.

   How many apples did she have left?

   She had _____ apples left.

10. Bonita gave 6 balloons to her friends.

    She had 9 balloons left.

    How many balloons did she have at first?

    She had _____ balloons at first.

11. Mrs. Gray had 20 eggs.

    She used some eggs to bake cakes.

    She had 8 eggs left.

    How many eggs did she use?

    She used _____ eggs.

EXERCISE 46

1. Match.

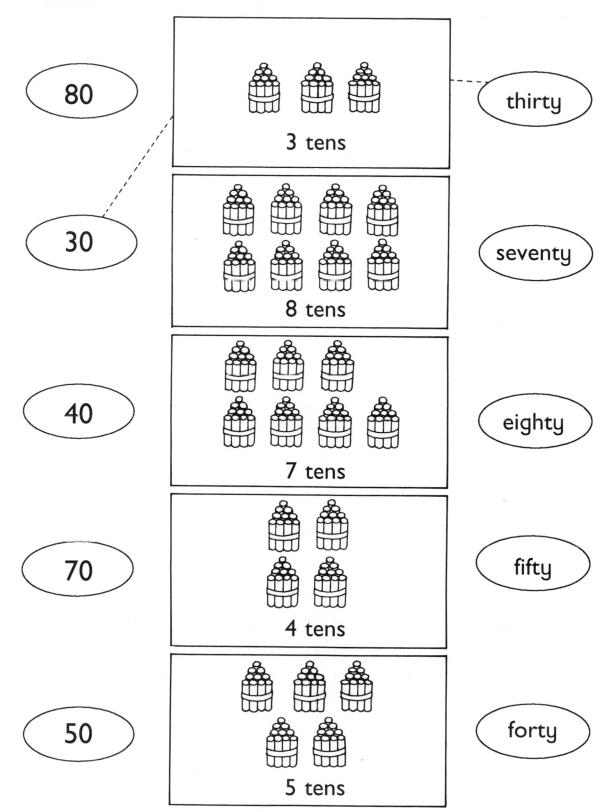

2. Write how many tens. Then write the number.

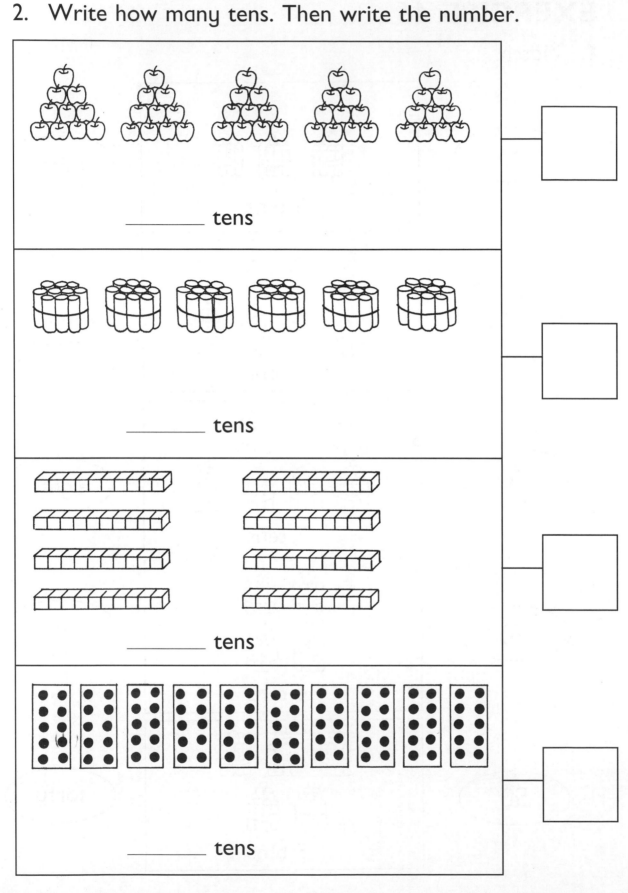

_____ tens

_____ tens

_____ tens

_____ tens

3. Write the numbers.

sixty

60

twenty

ninety

eighty

ten

thirty

fifty

one hundred

seventy

forty

117

EXERCISE 47

1. Match.

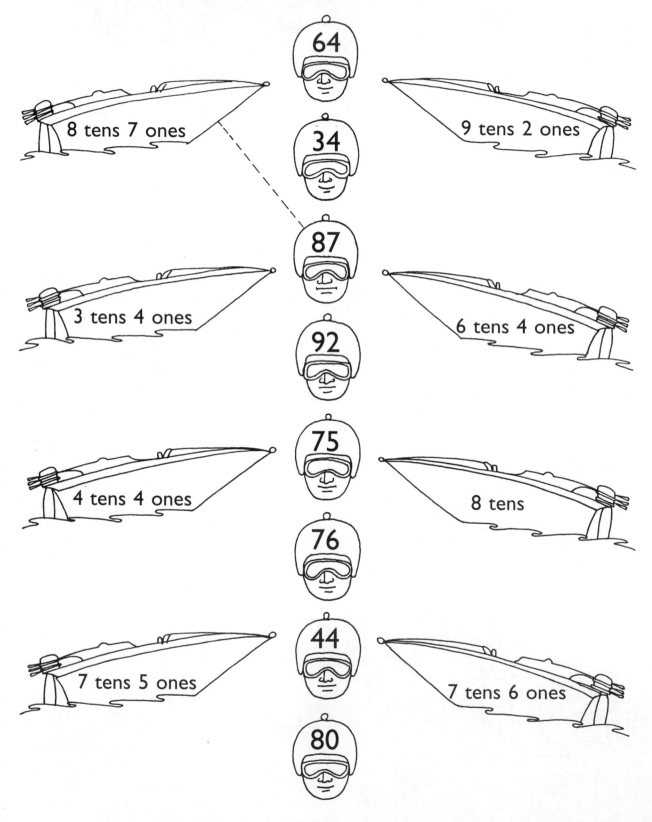

8 tens 7 ones

9 tens 2 ones

64

34

87

3 tens 4 ones

6 tens 4 ones

92

4 tens 4 ones

8 tens

75

76

7 tens 5 ones

7 tens 6 ones

44

80

2. Color the correct number.

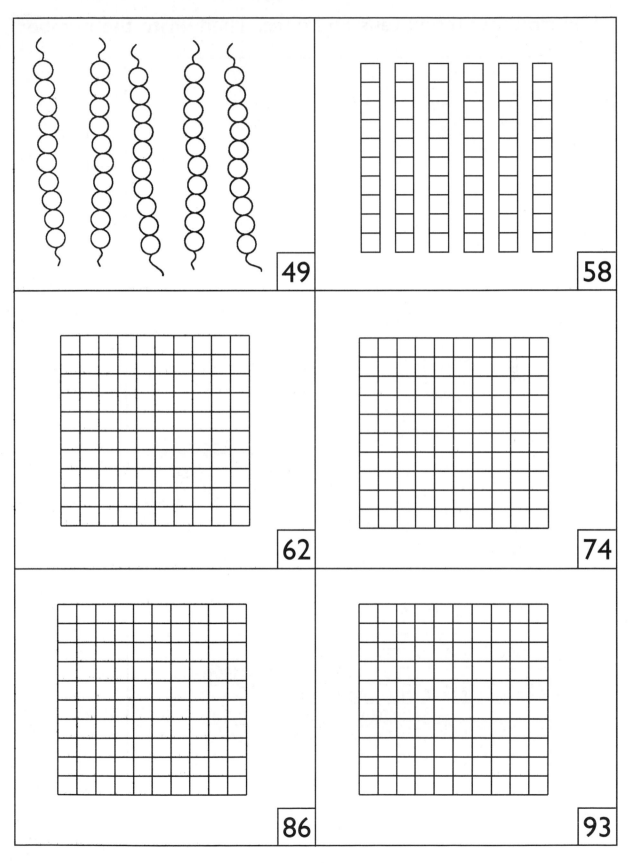

EXERCISE 48

1. Write how many tens and ones. Then write the number.

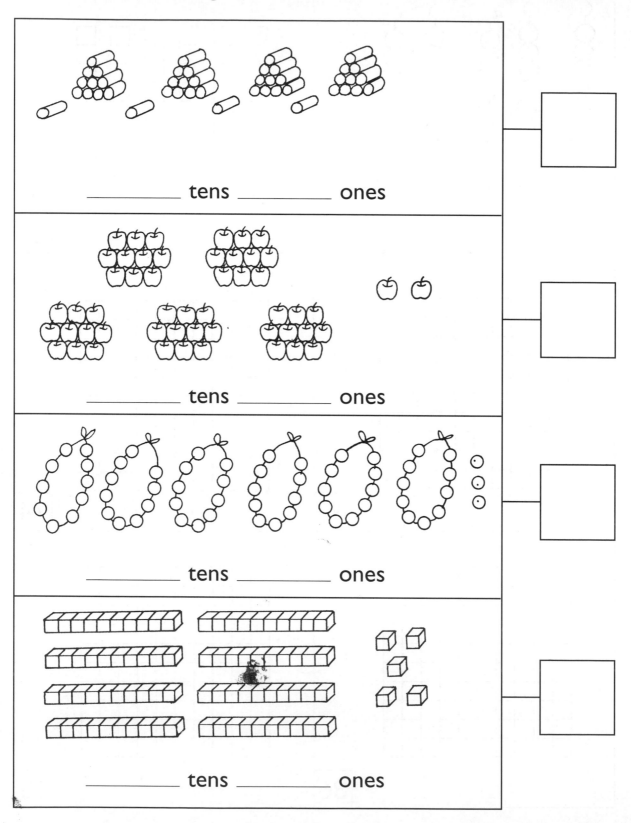

_____ tens _____ ones

_____ tens _____ ones

_____ tens _____ ones

_____ tens _____ ones

2. Write how many tens and ones. Then write the number.

(a)

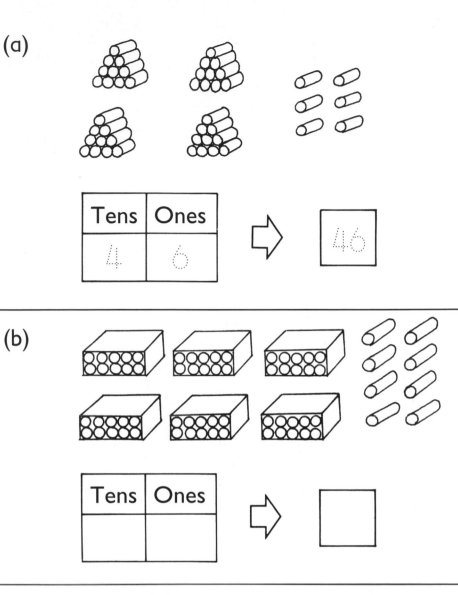

Tens	Ones
4	6

⇨ 46

(b)

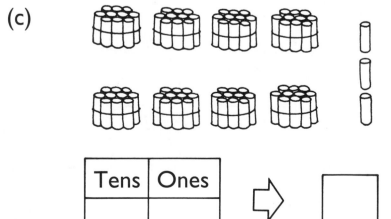

Tens	Ones

⇨

(c)

Tens	Ones

⇨

EXERCISE 49

1. Match.

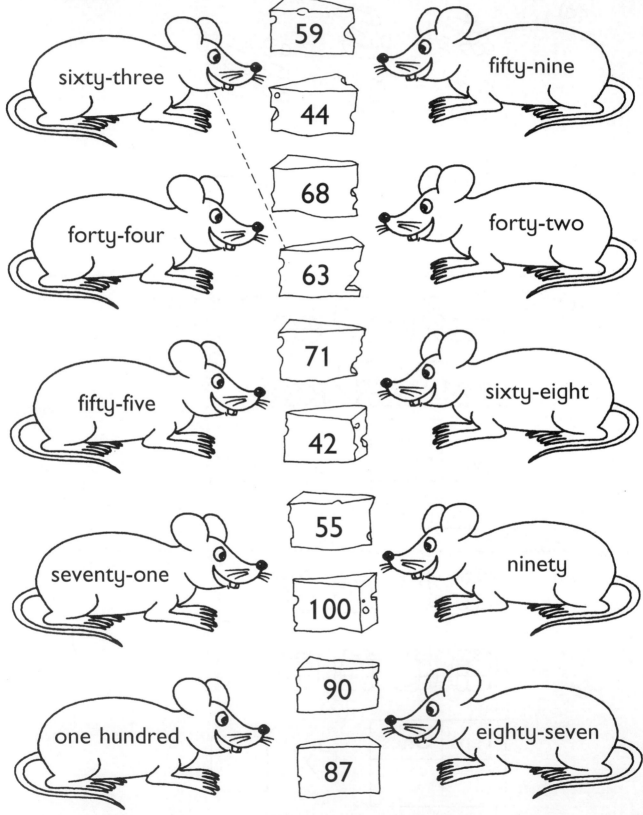

2. Write the numbers.

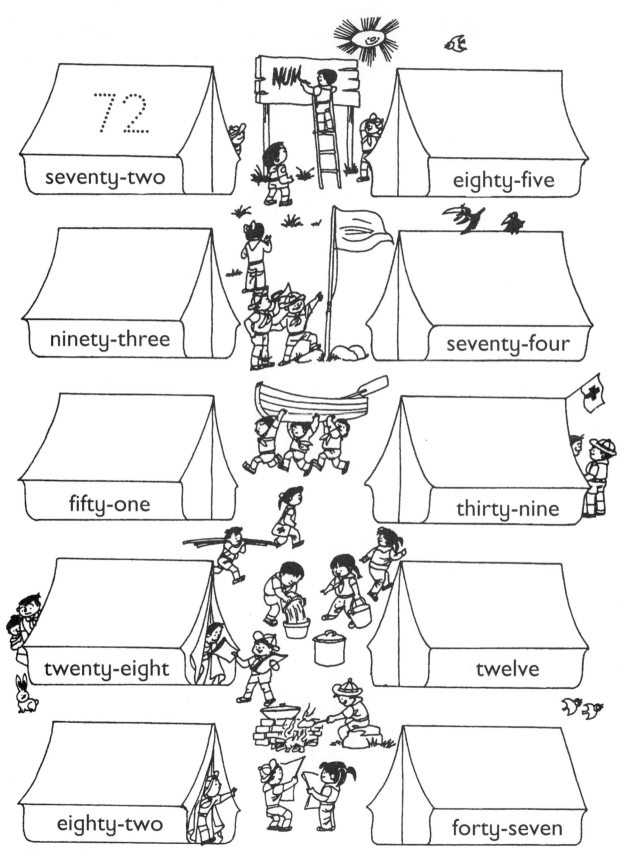

seventy-two

eighty-five

ninety-three

seventy-four

fifty-one

thirty-nine

twenty-eight

twelve

eighty-two

forty-seven

EXERCISE 50

1. Fill in the missing numbers.

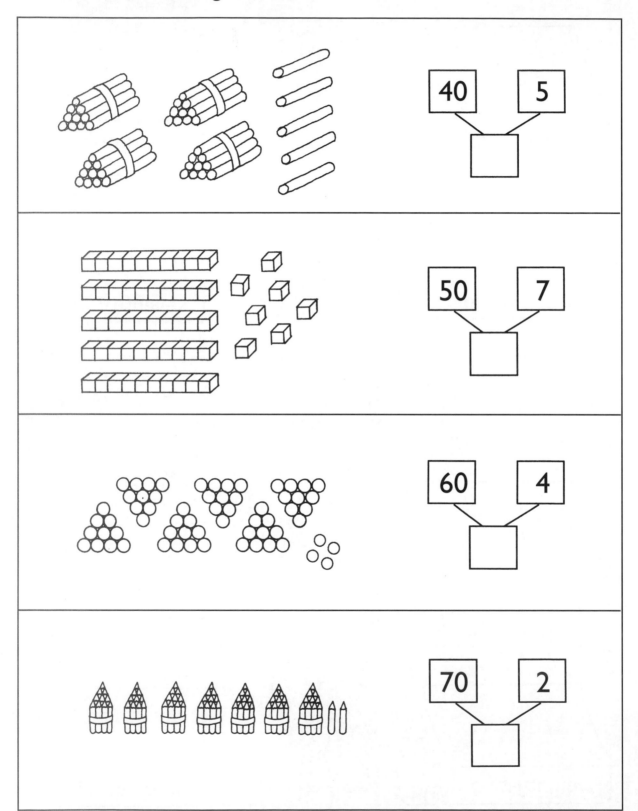

2. Add.

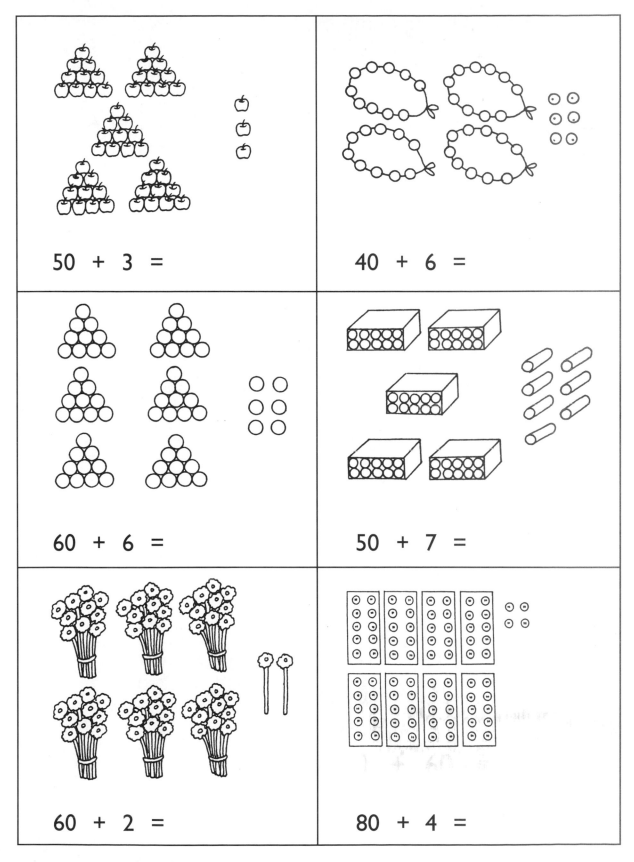

50 + 3 =

40 + 6 =

60 + 6 =

50 + 7 =

60 + 2 =

80 + 4 =

125

EXERCISE 51

1. Write the missing numbers.

(a)

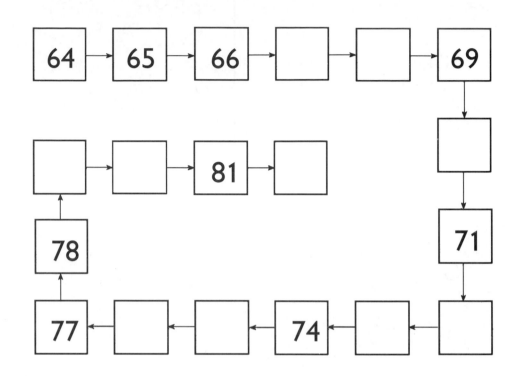

(b)

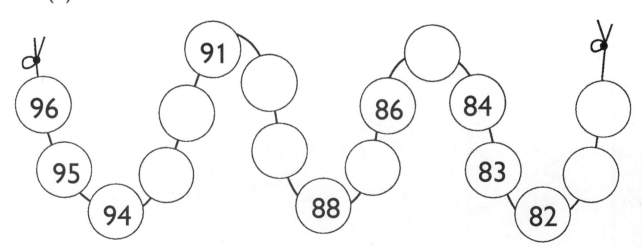

EXERCISE 52

1. Write the numbers in order. Begin with the given number.

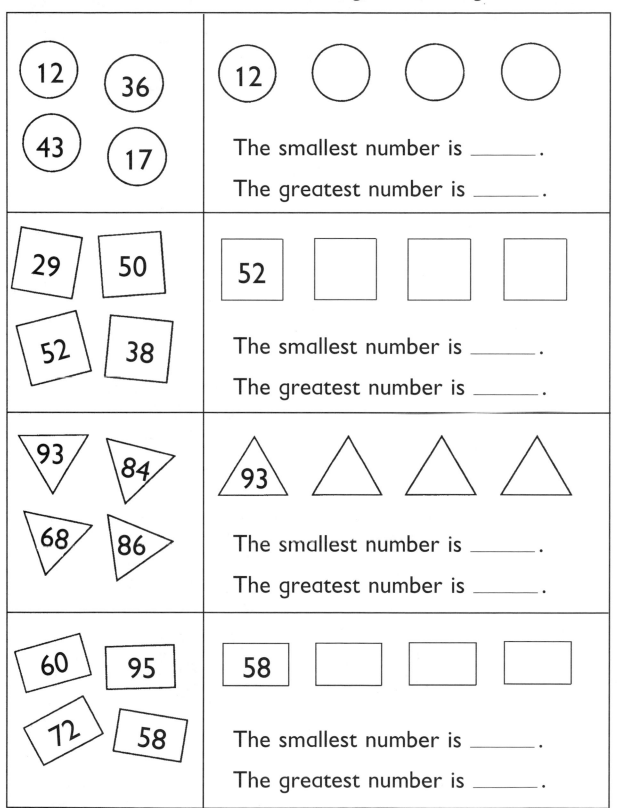

12   36
43   17

12 ◯ ◯ ◯

The smallest number is _____ .

The greatest number is _____ .

29   50
52   38

52 ☐ ☐ ☐

The smallest number is _____ .

The greatest number is _____ .

93   84
68   86

93 △ △ △

The smallest number is _____ .

The greatest number is _____ .

60   95
72   58

58 ☐ ☐ ☐

The smallest number is _____ .

The greatest number is _____ .

EXERCISE 53

1. Fill in the blanks.

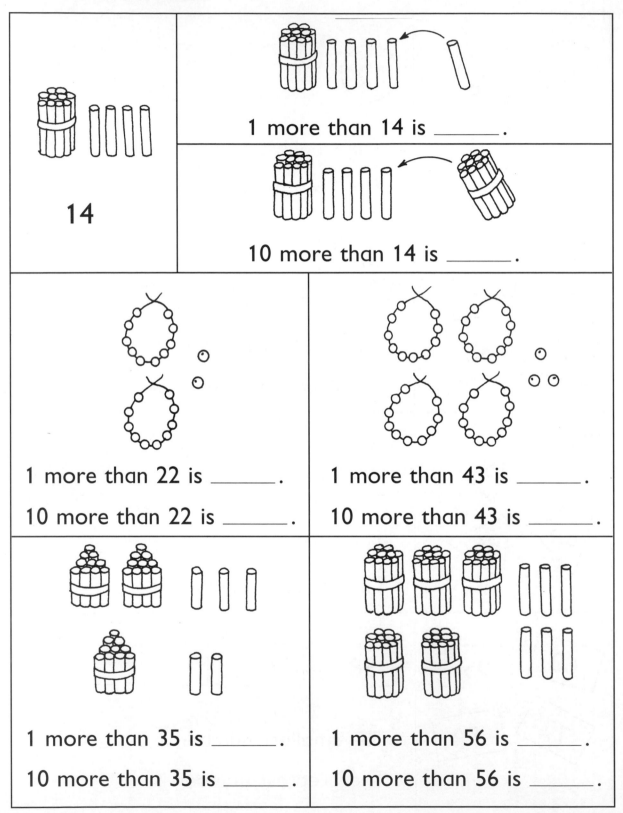

14

1 more than 14 is _____ .

10 more than 14 is _____ .

1 more than 22 is _____ .

10 more than 22 is _____ .

1 more than 43 is _____ .

10 more than 43 is _____ .

1 more than 35 is _____ .

10 more than 35 is _____ .

1 more than 56 is _____ .

10 more than 56 is _____ .

2. Fill in the blanks.

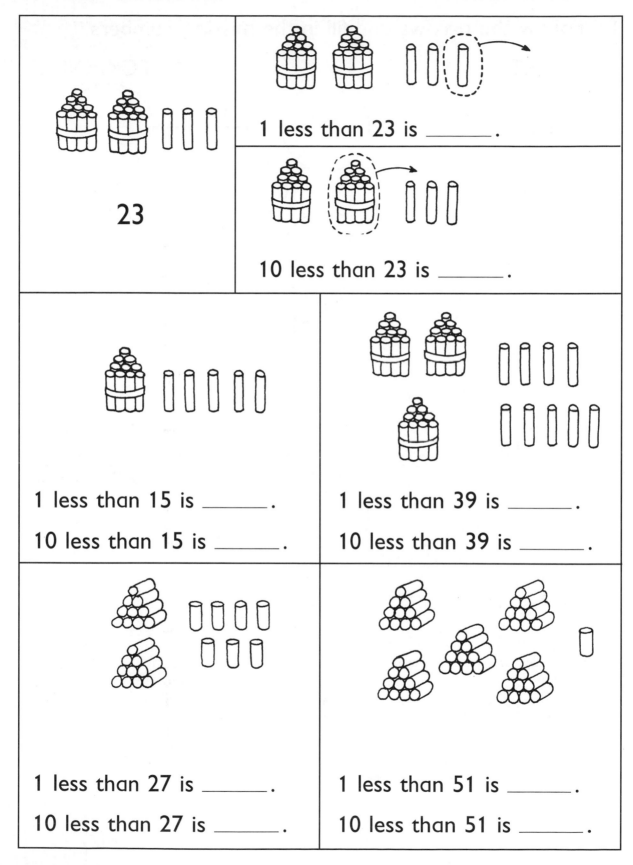

23

1 less than 23 is _____.

10 less than 23 is _____.

1 less than 15 is _____.

10 less than 15 is _____.

1 less than 39 is _____.

10 less than 39 is _____.

1 less than 27 is _____.

10 less than 27 is _____.

1 less than 51 is _____.

10 less than 51 is _____.

EXERCISE 54

1. Follow the arrows and fill in the missing numbers.

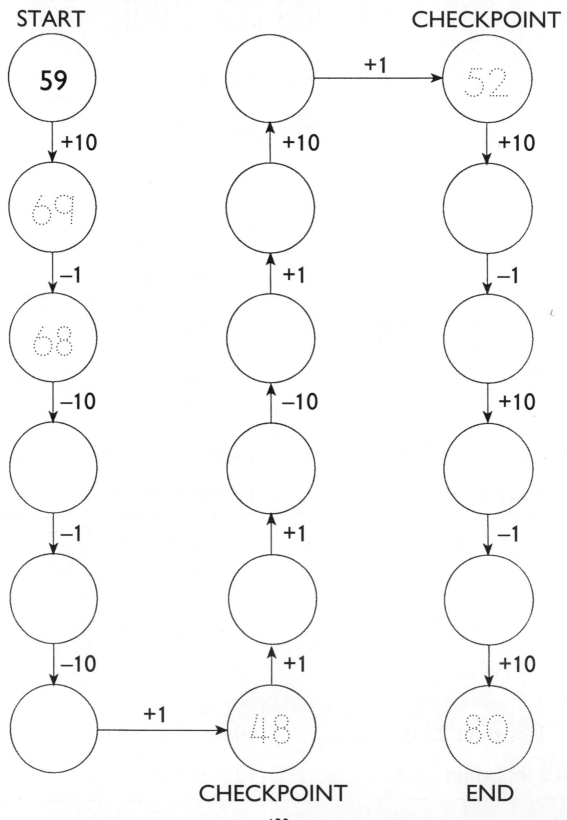

START

CHECKPOINT

59

+10

69

−1

68

−10

−1

−10

+1

CHECKPOINT

48

+1

+1

−10

+1

+1

+10

+1

52

+10

−1

+10

−1

+10

80

END

EXERCISE 55

1.

1	2	3	4	5	6	7	8	9	10
11	12	13	14	15	16	17	18	19	20
21	22	23	24	25	26	27	28	29	30
31	32	33	34	35	36	37	38	39	40
41	42	43	44	45	46	47	48	49	50
51	52	53	54	55	56	57	58	59	60
61	62	63	64	65	66	67	68	69	70
71	72	73	74	75	76	77	78	79	80
81	82	83	84	85	86	87	88	89	90
91	92	93	94	95	96	97	98	99	100

+1

−1

+10

−10

(a) 45 + 10 = ☐

Count on 1 ten from 45.

(b) 39 + 30 = ☐

Count on 3 tens from 39.

(c) 95 − 20 = ☐

Count backwards 2 tens from 95.

(d) 68 − 2 = ☐

Count backwards 2 ones fom 68.

(e) 71 + 3 = ☐

Count on 3 ones from 71.

(f) 56 − 30 = ☐

Count backwards 3 tens from 56.

(g) 87 − 3 = ☐

Count backwards 3 ones fom 87.

(h) 64 + 20 = ☐

Count on 2 tens from 64.

132

EXERCISE 56

1. Fill in the blanks.

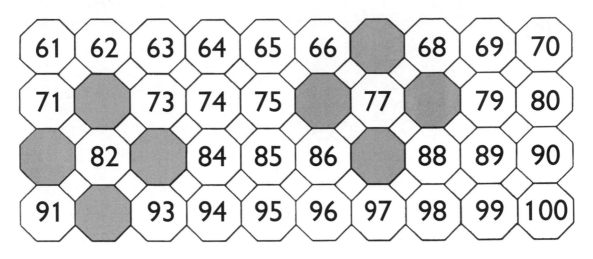

(a) 1 more than 77 is _____ .

(b) 10 more than 77 is _____ .

(c) 1 less than 82 is _____ .

(d) 10 less than 82 is _____ .

(e) 1 more than 80 is _____ .

(f) 2 less than 80 is _____ .

(g) 3 less than 84 is _____ .

(h) 10 less than 86 is _____ .

(i) 20 less than 98 is _____ .

(j) 30 more than 62 is _____ .

(k) 20 less than 96 is _____ .

EXERCISE 57

1. Add.

(a)

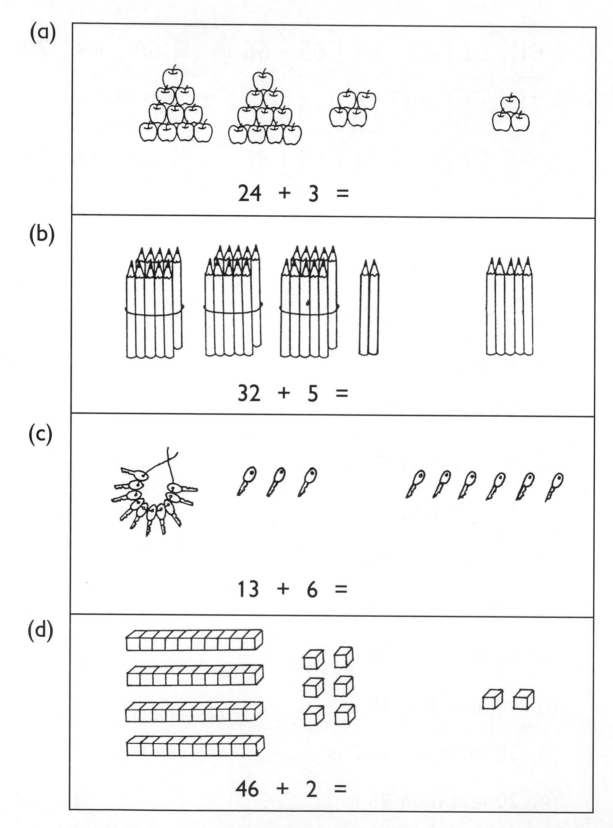

24 + 3 =

(b)

32 + 5 =

(c)

13 + 6 =

(d)

46 + 2 =

2. Add.

☐☐☐☐   ■■■

$4 + 3 = 7$

34 + 3 =

34 + 3
30   4

5 + 2 =	6 + 1 =
25 + 2 =	36 + 1 =
4 + 4 =	7 + 2 =
44 + 4 =	57 + 2 =
3 + 3 =	1 + 8 =
63 + 3 =	71 + 8 =

EXERCISE 58

1. Add.

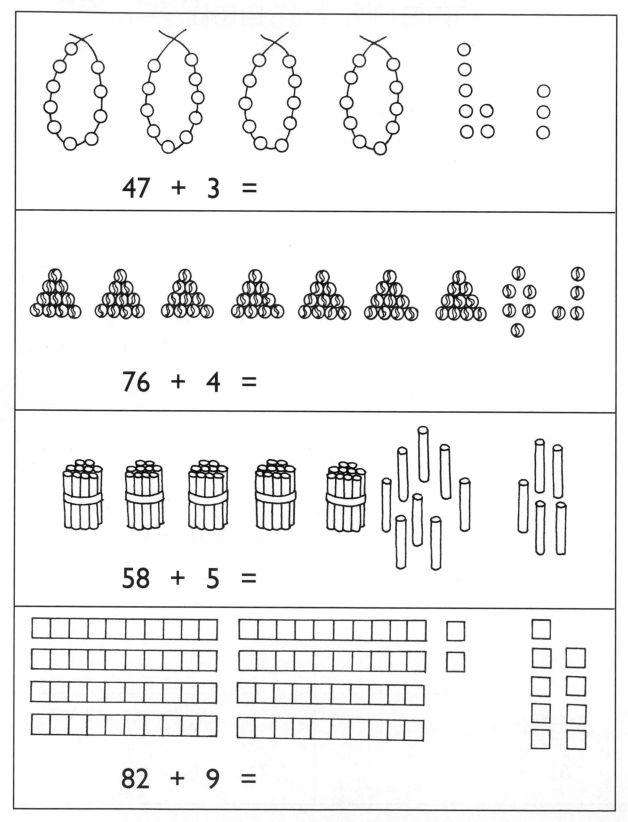

47 + 3 =

76 + 4 =

58 + 5 =

82 + 9 =

2. Add.

7 + 5 = 12

67 + 5 =

67 + 5

60   7

5 + 5 = 45 + 5 =	4 + 7 = 64 + 7 =
6 + 8 = 86 + 8 =	9 + 4 = 59 + 4 =
5 + 6 = 75 + 6 =	8 + 2 = 68 + 2 =

EXERCISE 59

1. Add.

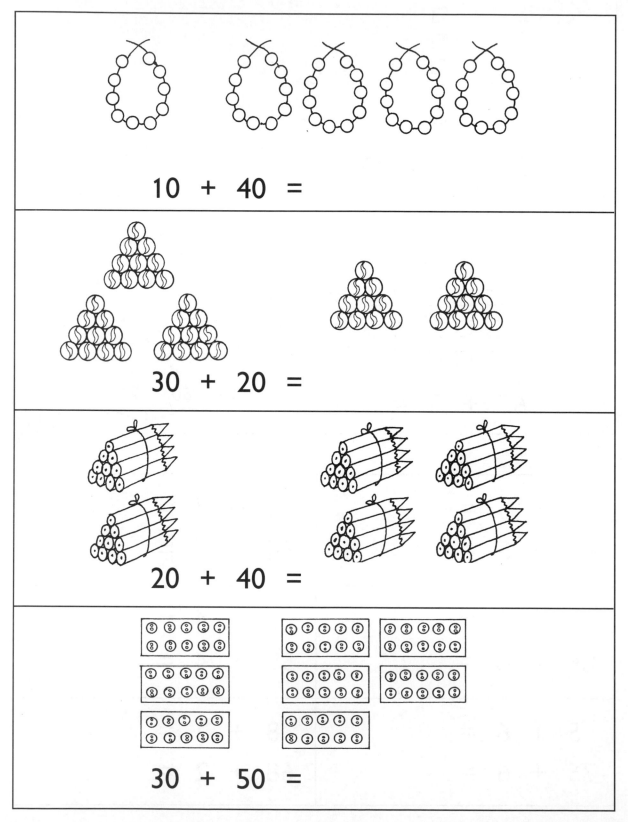

10 + 40 =

30 + 20 =

20 + 40 =

30 + 50 =

2. Add.

3 tens + 5 tens = _____ tens

30 + 50 = _____

---

2 tens + 3 tens = _____ tens

20 + 30 = _____

1 ten + 5 tens = _____ tens

10 + 50 = _____

---

3 tens + 4 tens = _____ tens

30 + 40 = _____

6 tens + 2 tens = _____ tens

60 + 20 = _____

---

2 tens + 7 tens = _____ tens

20 + 70 = _____

3 tens + 3 tens = _____ tens

30 + 30 = _____

---

8 tens + 1 ten = _____ tens

80 + 10 = _____

5 tens + 4 tens = _____ tens

50 + 40 = _____

EXERCISE 60

1. Add.

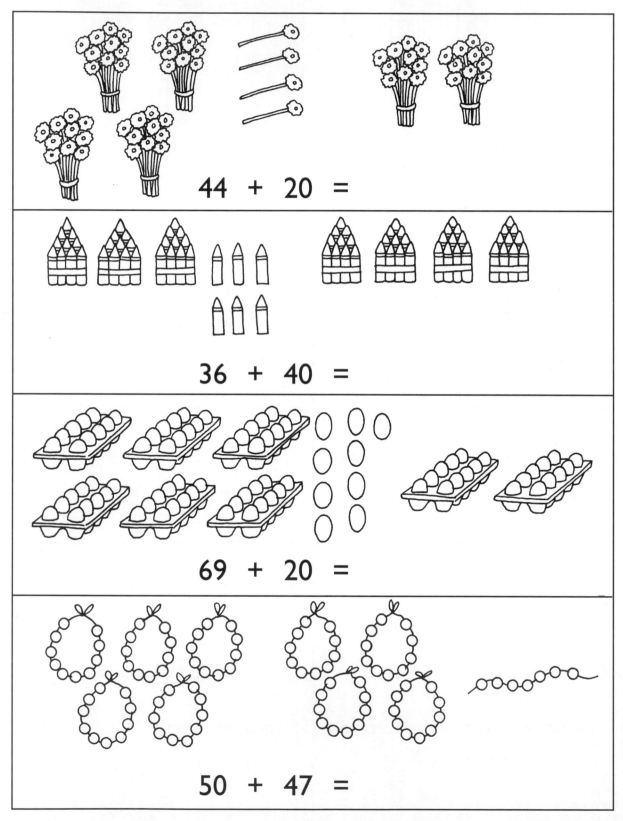

44 + 20 =

36 + 40 =

69 + 20 =

50 + 47 =

2. Add.

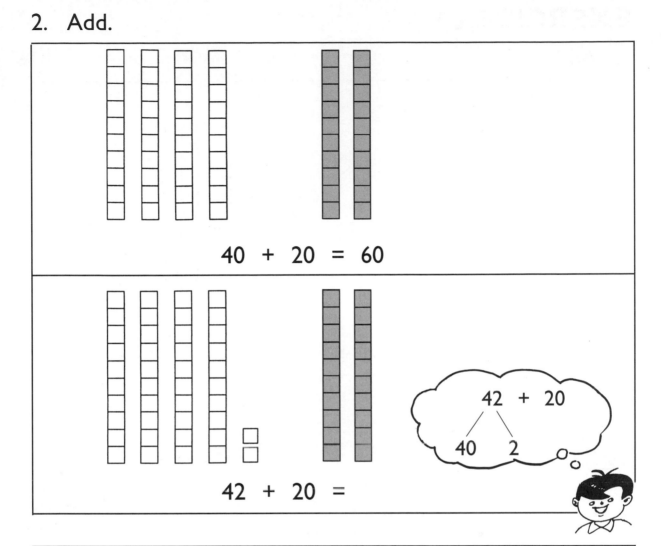

40 + 20 = 60

42 + 20 =

42 + 20
40   2

40 + 30 =	20 + 70 =
40 + 36 =	28 + 70 =
10 + 60 =	50 + 30 =
17 + 60 =	50 + 35 =
50 + 20 =	20 + 60 =
54 + 20 =	21 + 60 =

EXERCISE 61

1. Add.

$$25 + 14 =$$

$$25 + 10 + 4$$

$45 + 10 + 3 =$ $45 + 13 =$	$24 + 10 + 2 =$ $24 + 12 =$
$37 + 10 + 3 =$ $37 + 13 =$	$76 + 10 + 4 =$ $76 + 14 =$
$25 + 10 + 7 =$ $25 + 17 =$	$48 + 10 + 6 =$ $48 + 16 =$

2. Add.

$$33 + 25 =$$

33 + 20 + 5

42 + 30 + 6 = 42 + 36 =	35 + 40 + 2 = 35 + 42 =
55 + 20 + 5 = 55 + 25 =	28 + 60 + 2 = 28 + 62 =
37 + 30 + 8 = 37 + 38 =	65 + 20 + 9 = 65 + 29 =

EXERCISE 62

1. Subtract.

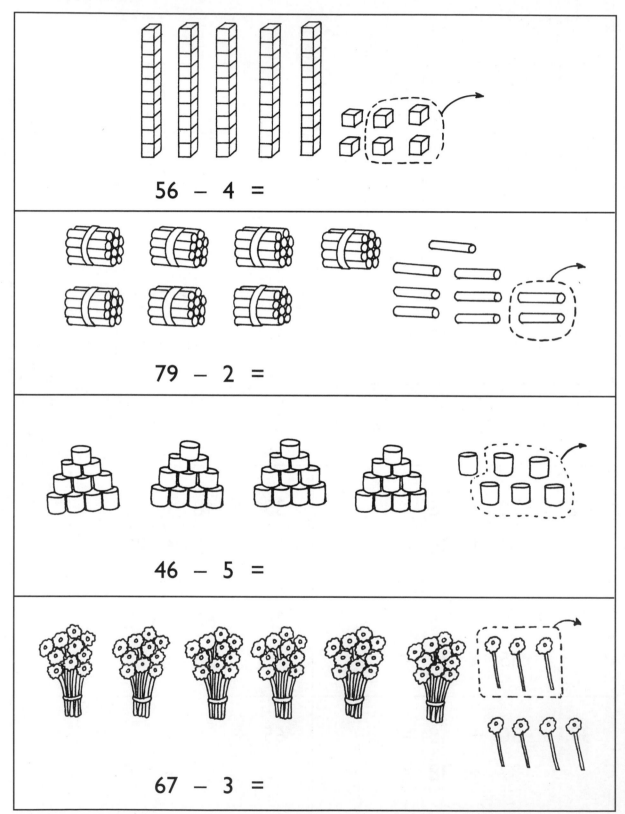

56 – 4 =

79 – 2 =

46 – 5 =

67 – 3 =

2. Subtract.

7 – 3 = 4

37 – 3 =

37 – 3
30   7

5 – 3 = 65 – 3 =	8 – 5 = 78 – 5 =
6 – 2 = 86 – 2 =	7 – 4 = 37 – 4 =
8 – 6 = 58 – 6 =	9 – 5 = 69 – 5 =

EXERCISE 63

1. Subtract.

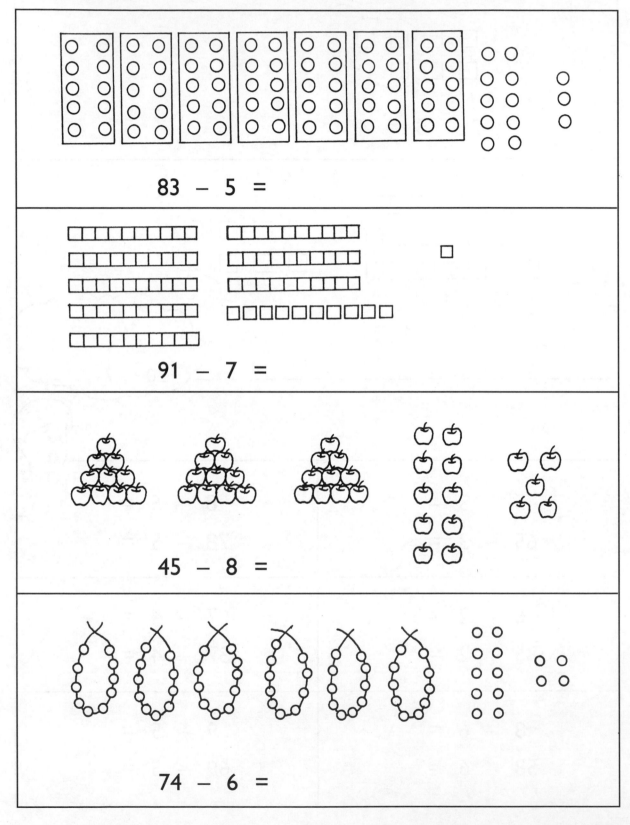

83 – 5 =

91 – 7 =

45 – 8 =

74 – 6 =

2. Subtract.

16 – 8 = 8

46 – 8 =

46 – 8
30   16

14 – 7 =
54 – 7 =

13 – 5 =
63 – 5 =

11 – 5 =
61 – 5 =

14 – 9 =
74 – 9 =

12 – 7 =
82 – 7 =

13 – 6 =
93 – 6 =

EXERCISE 64

1. Subtract.

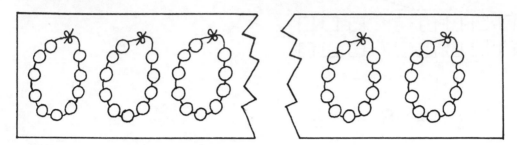

50 – 20 =

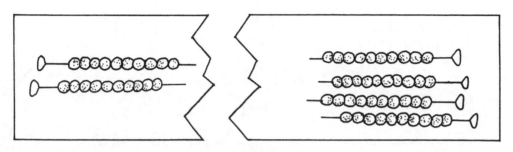

60 – 40 =

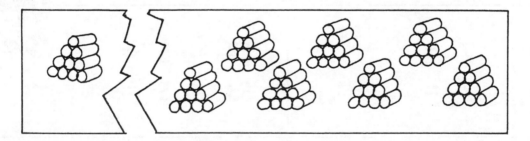

80 – 70 =

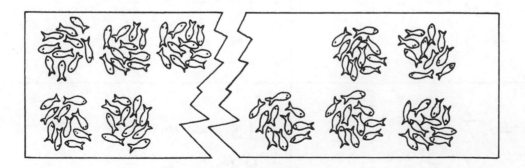

100 – 50 =

2. Subtract.

6 tens − 2 tens =

60 − 20   =

4 tens − 1 ten = _____ tens 40 − 10 = _____	5 tens − 3 tens = _____ tens 50 − 30 = _____
6 tens − 5 tens = _____ ten 60 − 50 = _____	7 tens − 4 tens = _____ tens 70 − 40 = _____
8 tens − 6 tens = _____ tens 80 − 60 = _____	7 tens − 2 tens = _____ tens 70 − 20 = _____
9 tens − 4 tens = _____ tens 90 − 40 = _____	10 tens − 7 tens = _____ tens 100 − 70 = _____

EXERCISE 65

1. Subtract.

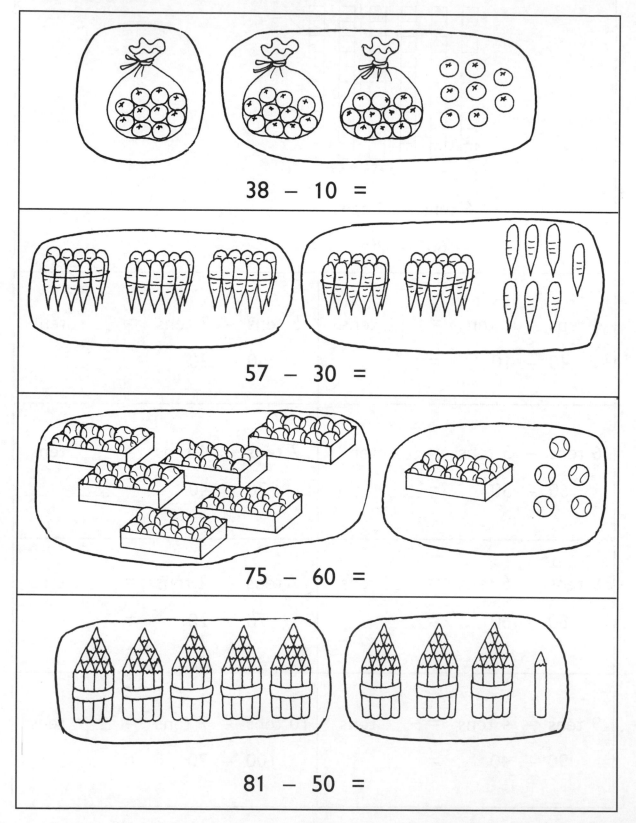

38 – 10 =

57 – 30 =

75 – 60 =

81 – 50 =

2. Subtract.

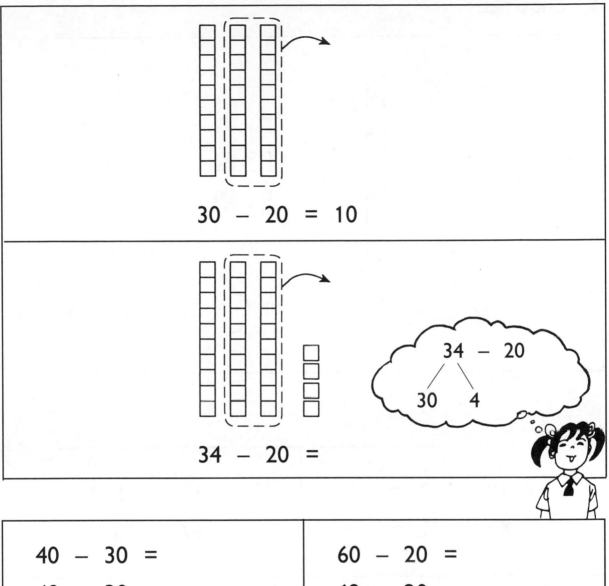

$$30 - 20 = 10$$

$$34 - 20 =$$

34 − 20

30   4

40 − 30 =	60 − 20 =
49 − 30 =	62 − 20 =
30 − 10 =	80 − 40 =
36 − 10 =	83 − 40 =
50 − 40 =	90 − 80 =
57 − 40 =	95 − 80 =

EXERCISE 66

1. Subtract.

36 – 13 =

36 – 10 – 3

47 – 10 – 2 = 47 – 12 =	67 – 10 – 5 = 67 – 15 =
58 – 10 – 8 = 58 – 18 =	60 – 10 – 4 = 60 – 14 =
43 – 10 – 7 = 43 – 17 =	61 – 10 – 3 = 61 – 13 =

2. Subtract.

46 − 22 =

46 − 20 − 2

68 − 20 − 4 = 68 − 24 =	75 − 40 − 2 = 75 − 42 =
53 − 30 − 3 = 53 − 33 =	60 − 20 − 8 = 60 − 28 =
73 − 40 − 7 = 73 − 47 =	96 − 80 − 7 = 96 − 87 =

REVIEW 6

1. Count the tens and ones.

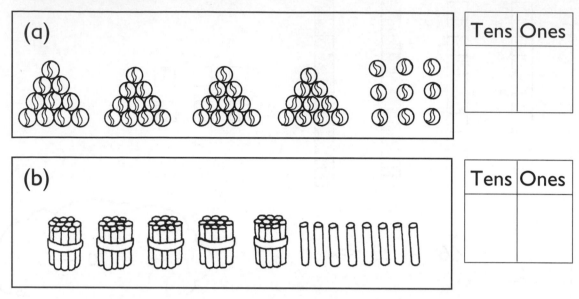

(a)

Tens	Ones

(b)

Tens	Ones

2. Fill in the missing numbers.

(a) 40 — 50 — ☐ — 70 — ☐ — 90 — ☐

(b) 6 — 8 — ☐ — ☐ — 14 — 16 — ☐ — ☐

(c) 40 — 35 — ☐ — ☐ — ☐ — 15 — 10 — 5

3. Arrange these numbers in order.

   Begin with the smallest.

☐ ☐ ☐ ☐ ☐

smallest   greatest

4. How many oranges are there altogether?

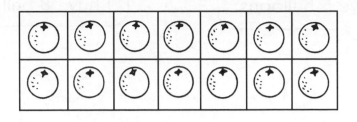

$7 \times 2 =$

There are _____ oranges altogether.

---

5. Share 8 balloons equally between 2 children.

   How many balloons does each child get?

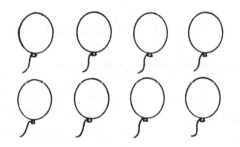

Each child gets _____ balloons.

---

6. Circle groups of 6 marbles.

   How many groups are there?

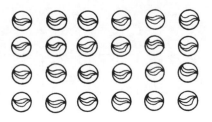

There are _____ groups.

7.

How many fewer balloons does David have than Lynn?

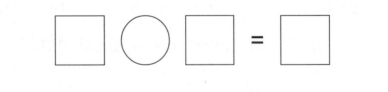

David has _____ fewer balloons than Lynn.

8.

How many cookies did Cameron eat?

Cameron ate _____ cookies.

9. There are 20 children in an art class.

   6 of them are girls.

   How many boys are there?

   There are _____ boys.

10. There are 8 big balls and 6 small balls in a basket.

    How many balls are there in the basket?

    There are _____ balls in the basket.

11. There are 15 marbles.

    4 of them are outside the bag.

    How many marbles are there in the bag?

    There are _____ marbles in the bag.

EXERCISE 67

1. Match.

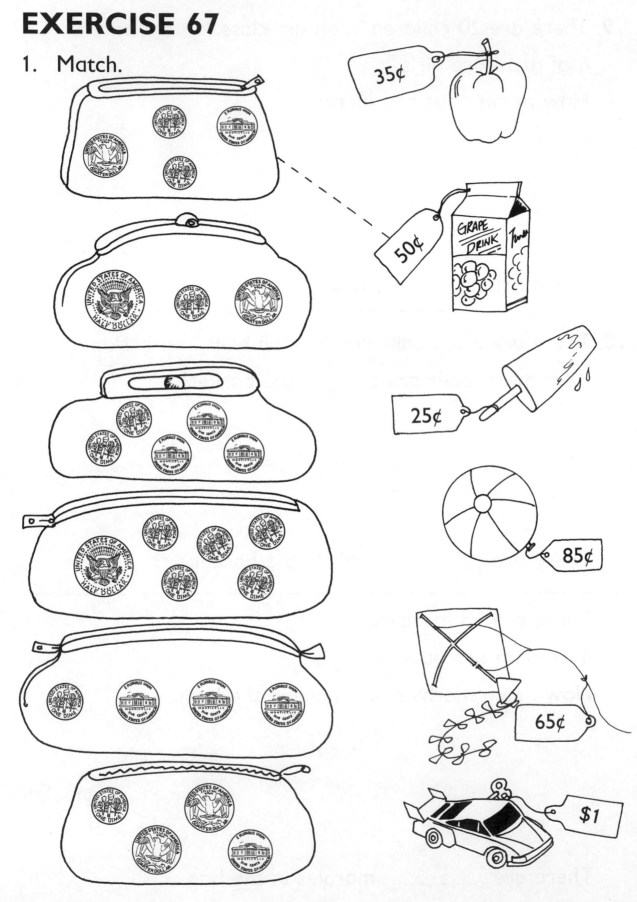

2. How much money is there in each set of coins?

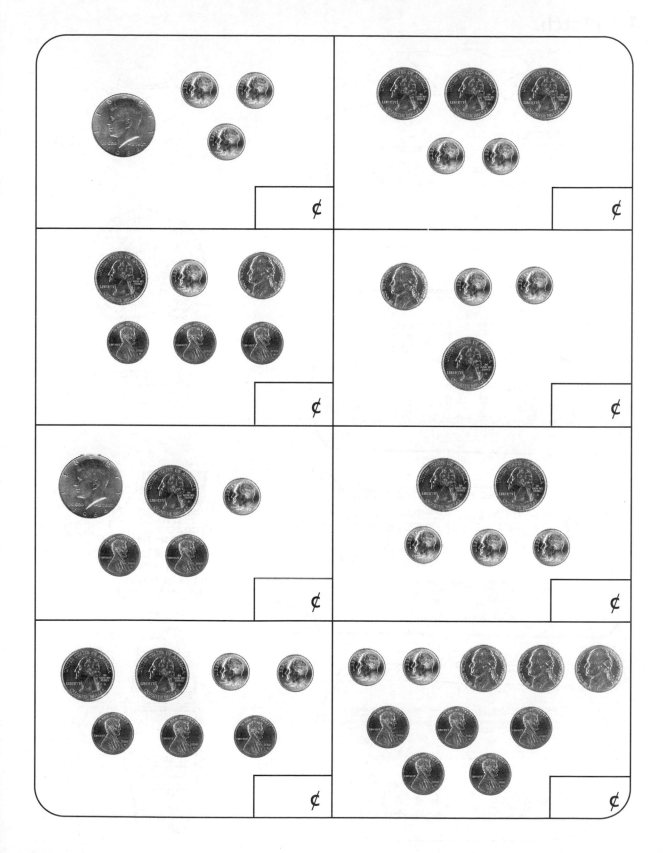

¢

¢

¢

¢

¢

¢

¢

¢

EXERCISE 68

1. Match.

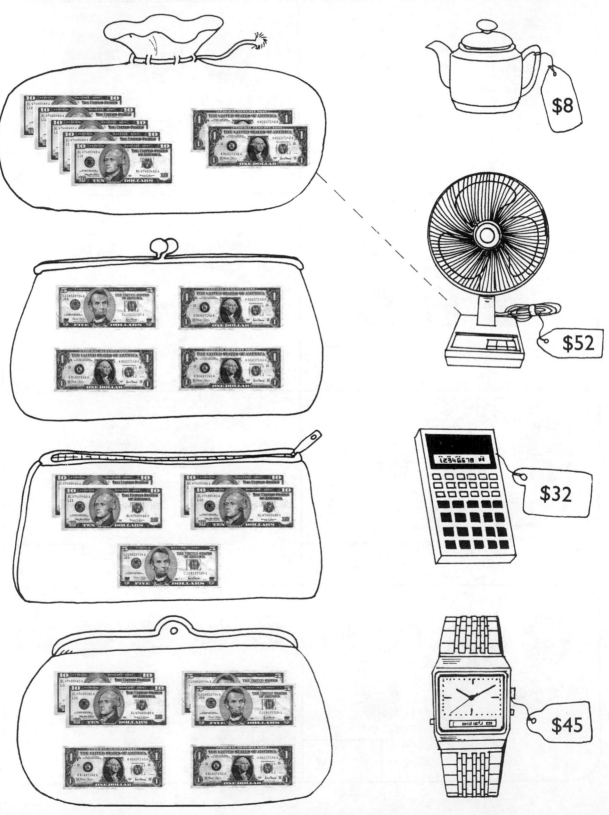

2. Color the correct amount of money.

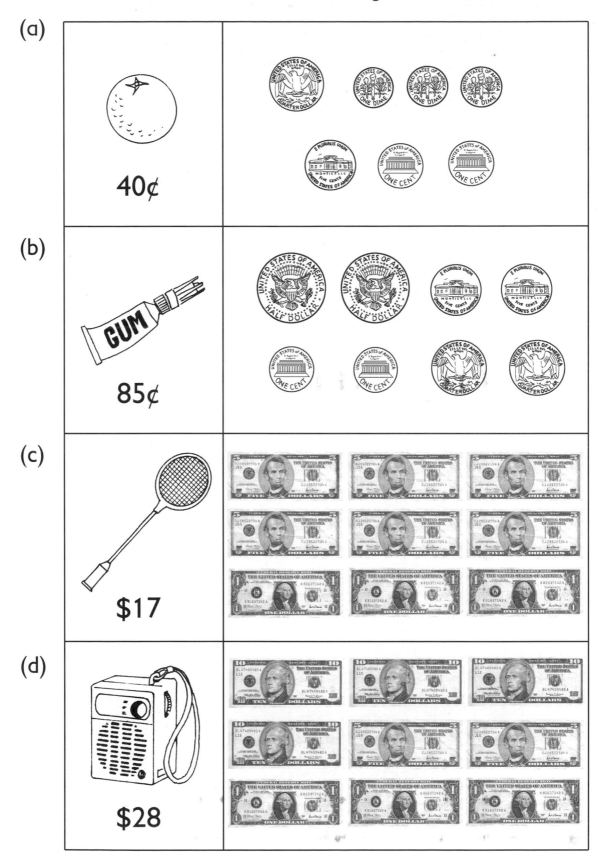

EXERCISE 69

1. Check ☑ the set that has more money.

(a)

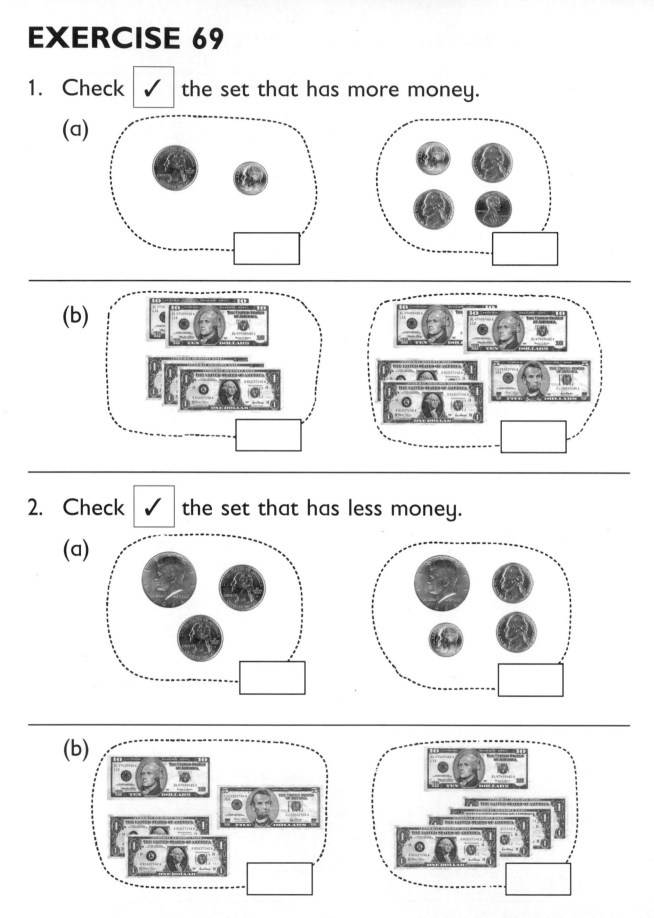

(b)

2. Check ☑ the set that has less money.

(a)

(b)

3. Check ✓ the set that has the most money.

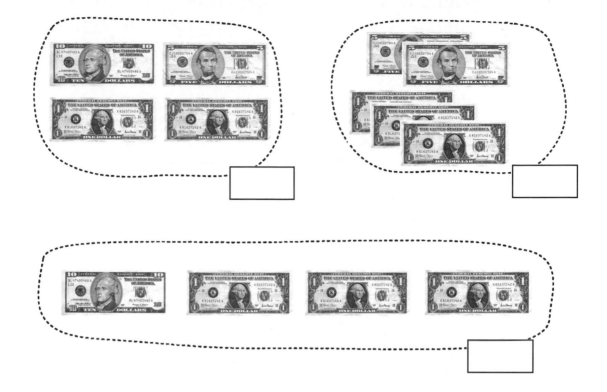

4. Check ✓ the set that has the least money.

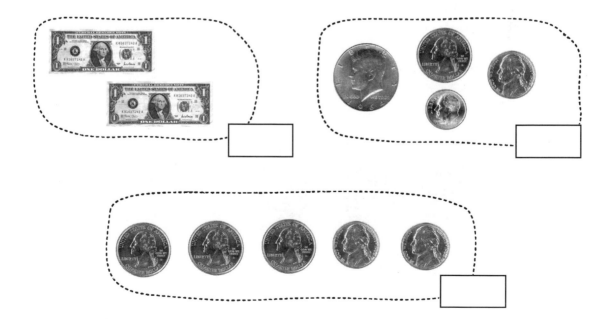

EXERCISE 70

1. Is the amount of money enough to buy the item?
   Write Yes or No.

(a)

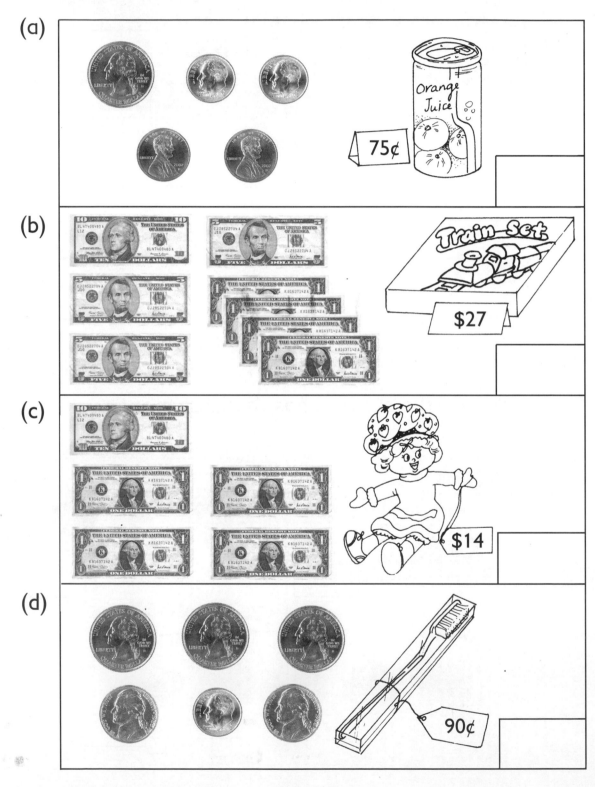

(b)

(c)

(d)

2. Mr. Brown had $20.

   He bought the watch.

   How much money did he have left?

   $13

   $20 − $13 =

   He had $ _____ left.

3.

   $12

   Juan has $9.

   He wants to buy the toy camera.

   How much more money does he need?

   $12 − $9 =

   He needs $ _____ more.

4. (a) Devi has 55¢.
   She wants to buy the pen.
   She needs _____ ¢ more.

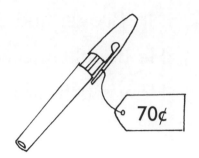
70¢

(b) Morgan had $1.
   She bought the toy boat.
   She had _____ ¢ left.

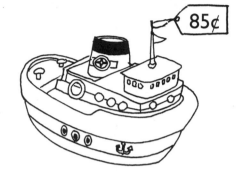
85¢

(c) Sara bought two pears.
   She paid _____ ¢.

40¢ each

(d) Brian spent $1.
   He bought the _____ and
   the _____ .

ice-cream

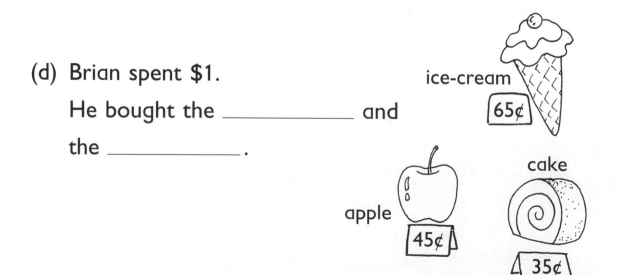
65¢

apple
45¢

cake
35¢

REVIEW 7

1. Match.

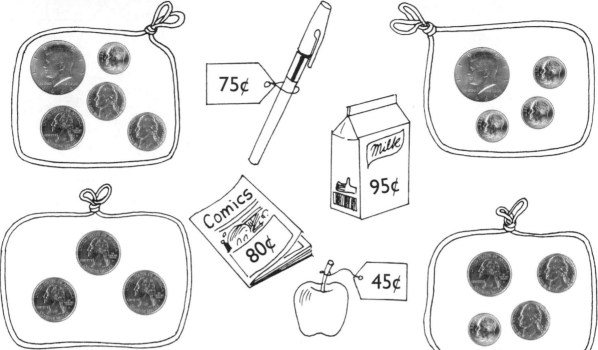

2. How much money is there in each set?

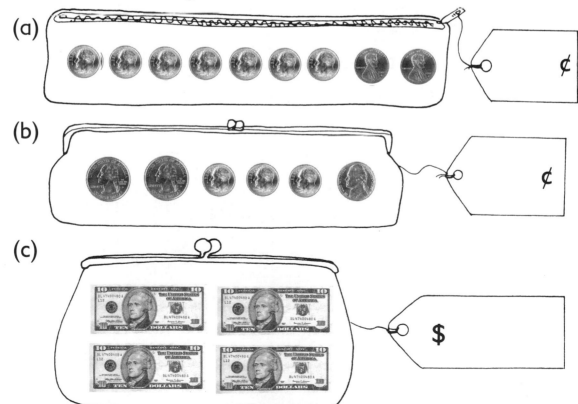

(a) _____ ¢

(b) _____ ¢

(c) $ _____

3.

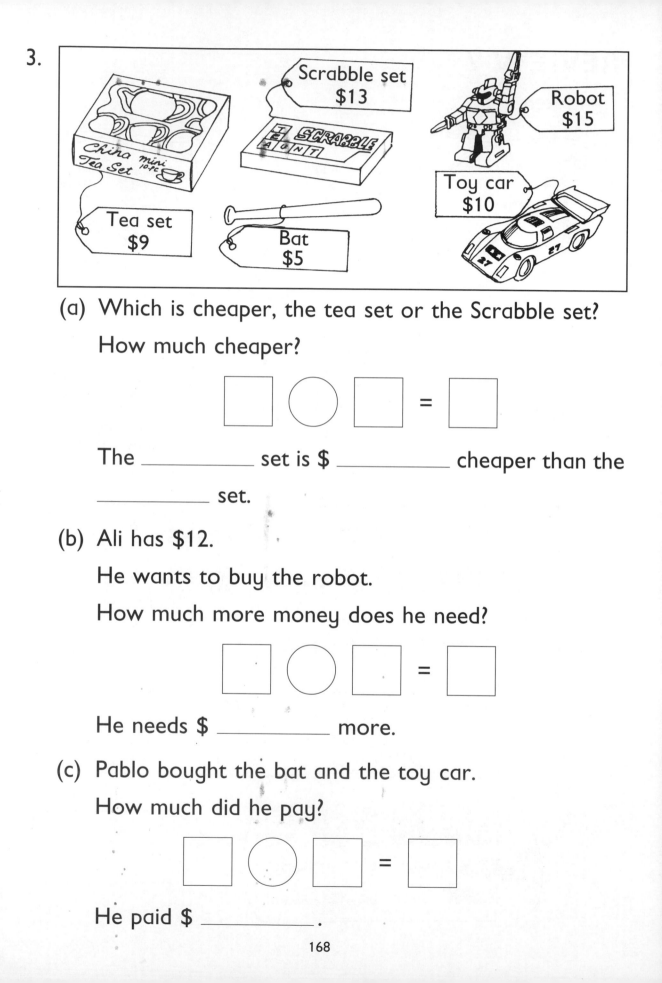

(a) Which is cheaper, the tea set or the Scrabble set?

How much cheaper?

$$\boxed{}\ \bigcirc\ \boxed{}\ =\ \boxed{}$$

The _____ set is $ _____ cheaper than the

_____ set.

(b) Ali has $12.

He wants to buy the robot.

How much more money does he need?

$$\boxed{}\ \bigcirc\ \boxed{}\ =\ \boxed{}$$

He needs $ _____ more.

(c) Pablo bought the bat and the toy car.

How much did he pay?

$$\boxed{}\ \bigcirc\ \boxed{}\ =\ \boxed{}$$

He paid $ _____ .

4.

I bought 3 mangoes.

I bought 10 mangoes.

Mr. Lee

Mr. Garcia

Who bought more mangoes? How many more?

| | ◯ | | = | |

Mr. _____ bought _____ more mangoes than

Mr. _____ .

5.

I have 13 marbles.

I have 7 more marbles than Ryan.

Ryan

Peter

How many marbles does Peter have?

| | ◯ | | = | |

Peter has _____ marbles.

6. After giving away 5 shells, John had 6 shells left.

   How many shells did he have at first?

   He had _____ shells at first.

7. Nicole bought 12 pastries.

   She put 4 of them on a plate.

   She put the rest in a box.

   How many pastries were there in the box?

   There were _____ pastries in the box.

8. Mary has 11 story books.

   She has 2 more story books than Sally.

   How many story books does Sally have?

   Sally has _____ story books.

REVIEW 8

1. Follow the arrows and fill in the missing numbers.

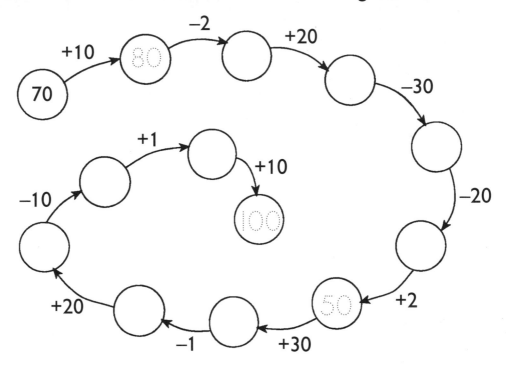

2. Add or subtract.

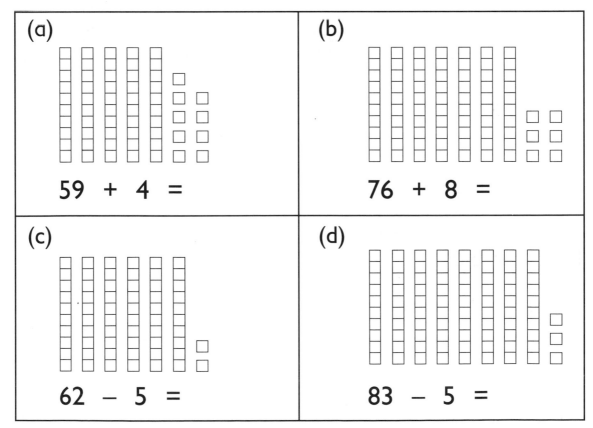

(a)

59 + 4 =

(b)

76 + 8 =

(c)

62 − 5 =

(d)

83 − 5 =

3. Color the 3 pieces that form the given square.

4. Color a half of the square.

   Color a quarter of the rectangle.

Ryan's Toys

Boat	Car	Airplane	Soldier

Each ⬤ stands for 1 toy.

Fill in the blanks.

(a) Ryan has _____ airplanes.

(b) He has _____ more boats than cars.

(c) He has _____ fewer soldiers than airplanes.

(d) He has _____ toys altogether.

6.

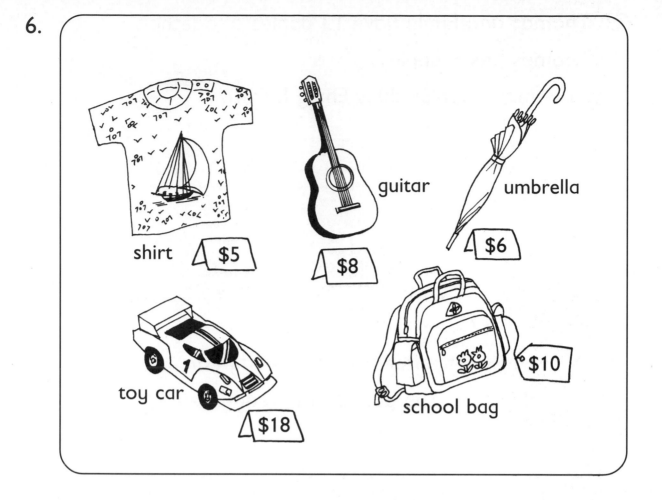

guitar

umbrella

shirt $5

$8

$6

toy car

school bag

$18

$10

(a) Devi bought the guitar and the umbrella.

She spent $ _____ altogether.

(b) Rahmat had $20.

He bought the toy car.

He had $ _____ left.

(c) The school bag is $ _____ cheaper than the toy car.

(d) Meihua spent $13.

She bought the _____ and the _____ .

7. Thomas and Emily have 13 apples altogether.

   Thomas has 6 apples.

   How many apples does Emily have?

   Emily has _____ apples.

---

8. Sara had $20.

   She had $6 left after buying a teddy bar.

   How much did she pay for the teddy bear?

   She paid $ _____ for the teddy bear.

---

9. Justin has $11.

   He has $3 less than Tom.

   How much money does Tom have?

   Tom has $ _____ .

174

10. Amy has 32 stickers.
Lacey gives her 23 more.
How many stickers does Amy have now?

Amy has _____ stickers now.

---

11. There are 3 dimes and 3 nickels in a purse.
What is the total amount of cents in the purse?

The total amount of cents in the purse is _____.

---

12. Mary has a dollar bill.
How many quarters can she get for the dollar bill?

Mary can get _____ quarters.

13. Peter has 3 nickels. John has 2 dimes. David has 1 quarter.
    Who has the most money?

    _____ has the most money.

14. Adam paid 3 quarters and 1 nickel for a candy bar.
    How much did the candy bar cost?

    The candy bar cost _____ cents.

15. Juan has 54 marbles.
    He gives away 6 of them.
    How many marbles does he have left?

    He has _____ marbles left.